Know Your Future

Thai Astrology
Step by Step

JOHN HUNT PUBLISHING

First published by O-Books, 2010
O-Books is an imprint of John Hunt Publishing Ltd., 3 East St., Alresford,
Hampshire SO24 9EE, UK
office@jhpbooks.com
www.johnhuntpublishing.com
www.o-books.com

For distributor details and how to order please visit the 'Ordering' section on our website.

Text copyright: Thirachai Phuvanatnaranubala
and Kornaek Khongpurttiroj 2009

ISBN: 978 1 84694 340 9

A CIP catalogue record for this book is available from the British Library.

Design: Stuart Davies

UK: Printed and bound by CPI Group (UK) Ltd, Croydon, CR0 4YY
Printed in North America by CPI GPS partners

We operate a distinctive and ethical publishing philosophy in
all areas of our business, from our global network of authors to
production and worldwide distribution.

Know Your Future

Thai Astrology
Step by Step

Thirachai Phuvanatnaranubala

&

Kornaek Khongpurttiroj

BOOKS

Winchester, UK
Washington, USA

CONTENTS

Introduction

Don't you want to know your own future?

This book is about Thai astrology. You will learn how to predict your own future by following only ten planets.

Astrology is a science that describes the influence of planets on man through statistics gathered over thousands of years. Planet positions at your birth time determine your habits, your behavior and your attitude to events. They, in turn, influence your potential future success and failure. Daily planet movements after your birth are predetermined and can be calculated in advance for hundreds of years. When they reach certain positions, their combination will maximize the possibility of certain aspects of your life happening, such as career success or failure, marriage or divorce, etc. By looking up the planet positions in advance, you can predict your own future.

Astrology is not against free will. Events will still happen, but you can modify your behavior to increase the chances and the level of success or lessen the risks and the impact of failure.

Why Thai astrology?

Thai astrology is very simple for laymen because the readings are done at more than one level. At the first few levels, the readings are broad-brushed, hence quite easy to use. You can apply them right away.

Thai astrology is based on Hindu Sidereal system. The lines dividing the Houses are fixed and are the same as the lines dividing the zodiac signs. Planet positions do not follow astronomy but are calculated from the formula of the ancient Hindu *Suriya Siddhanta* almanac. The dates of the sun changing zodiac signs therefore do not follow the seasons. The readings are not based on the actual angles between planets but instead on the relationship between the Houses. Planet diaries are available

1

on the website so readers can use them to predict their future.

However, Thai astrology is different from Indian in three ways. First, it uses round charts like Western astrology which is easier to understand than the Indian squares. Planets are represented by simple numbers so readers do not have to memorize zodiac symbols. Second, in Indian astrology, Rahu (8) is the ascending node of the Moon (2)'s orbit intersecting the celestial equator, and Ketu (9) is descending node. Thai astrology calculates the movement of Ketu (9) separately, making it more refined. Third, it uses the technique of Taksa (details in the book) which is unique to Thai astrology.

How to use this book

While the first few levels are easy to understand, the higher levels do require some concentration. We suggest for you to read through, even skipping some technical sections and go to the birth charts of famous people in order to get an overall view. This can make it easier when you go back to the technical parts.

Part I:

Astrology Communicates Through

the Position of the Planets

1. The Birth Chart

Producing a birth chart from the website

You can read this book as is. But you may find it more interesting with your own birth chart in hand as you read along. This book is aimed at laymen; therefore it does not describe how to manually construct a birth chart. You can produce your birth chart from the following website:

www.knowyourfuturethewebsite.com

The website will ask for your local birth date and local birth time, and the name of the town closest to where you were born. The computer program will automatically convert your birth date and birth time to the Thai time of GMT+07.00 and generate the birth chart. However, the automatic time conversion by the computer is done based on the unadjusted standard time of the town as selected by you. It will show such time in reference to GMT. For example, if you choose London, United Kingdom, it will display and use the time of GMT+00.00.

The program does not take into account day light saving time that is used in certain countries. Also, in some countries such adjustment was used only for a limited number of years in the past, and may have changed their time system since. You will have to make these specific time adjustment yourself manually, by putting in GMT plus or minus the number of hours. If you make the adjustment yourself, the program will use the manually adjusted GMT plus or minus time as the reference. It will still print out the information about the local birth date, local birth time and the town and country that you typed in for information.

When you are not sure about the specific time adjustment, we suggest that you put in two or three possible variations. The birth charts will have planets in slightly different positions, as well as the Lagna. You can then see which chart is correct.

What if I don't know the exact time of my birth?

If you don't know your exact time of birth, put in the nearest time that you know. At least it will generate a birth chart to which you can refer as you read along. If you just know the birth date but do not know the birth time at all, put in 12.00 AM noon of your birth date in order to produce a birth chart just for the purpose of reading this book. The position of the planets within a given day is mostly the same, except for the Moon (2) which is fast moving.

When you input 12.00 AM noon just to produce a birth chart, beware of the planet that is very close to the line dividing the zodiac signs (as indicated by the degrees and minutes). That planet can, in fact, be in either of the zodiac signs depending on the exact time of birth. For example, in the rough 12.00 AM birth chart, the position of Venus (6) may be at 29 degrees and 59 minutes in Aries. With the correct birth time (suppose it is late at night), Venus (6) could be in Taurus instead. Therefore, you should read Venus (6) in both signs.

Example of a birth chart

We believe this to be the birth chart of Diana the Princess of Wales, born on Saturday 1 July 1961 at 19.45 in Sandringham, United Kingdom, British Summer Time, GMT+01.00. She was married on 29 July 1981 and had 2 sons in 1982 and 1984. She was officially separated from her spouse in 1992 and officially divorced in 1996. She passed away on 31 August 1997.

We select her not only because most readers know her life story, but we also want the readers to see the link from her birth chart to those of Prince Charles and Prince William later in the book. The purpose is simply to show the technical side of the influence of the planets on one's life, and not to try to make any judgment whatsoever. We have not obtained official verification of the birth time of all the people involved, therefore cannot claim without any doubt that it is her birth chart.

The birth chart of Princess Diana

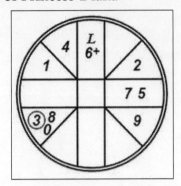

Thai astrology date: Saturday
Calendar Sunday 2 July 1961 at 01.45
Sunrise at 05.54

The planet table is as follow:

	Planet	Zodiac sign		Degree	Minute	R/S/F	Nawang	E
L	Lagna	0	Aires	0	0		1:03	E
1	Sun	2	Gemini	16	15		5:07	
2	Moon	10	Aquarius	0	3		1:06	E
3	Mars	4	Leo	8	55		3:04	
4	Mercury	1	Taurus	27	37		9:04	
5	Jupiter	9	Capricorn	14	10	R	5:06	
6	Venus	0	Aires	29	43		9:05	
7	Satum	9	Capricorn	0	7	R	1:07	E
8	Rahu	4	Leo	5	50		2:06	
9	Ketu	8	Sagittarius	12	53		4:02	
0	Uranus	4	Leo	2	11		1:03	E

Venus (6) is Tanu-set. Mars (3) is Tanu-kaset.

Saturn (7) is in Ruler position in Capricorn the 10th (Career) House.

Venus (6) is in Insecure position in Aires the 1st (Self) House

Rahu (8) is in Insecure position in Leo the 5th (Children) House

Jupiter (5) is in Fall position in Capricorn the 10th (Career) House

The Sun (1) is in Assistance position in Gemini the 3rd (Friend) House

Although Diana's birth time is converted into Thai time at 01.45, which is Sunday 2 July 1961 on the calendar, Thai astrology still considers it to be Saturday because day change is considered to be at 06:00 in Thailand. You can see in Diana's birth chart that the planets are numbered, as well as their locations in the chart. For convenience, instead of using astrological symbols for the planets, Thai astrology uses numbers as follow:

Planet	Number
The Sun	1
The Moon	2
Mars	3
Mercury	4
Jupiter	5
Venus	6
Saturn	7
Rahu	8
Ketu	9
Uranus	0

The Sun (1) is, of course, not a planet but the center of the solar system. However, ancient astrologers had found it to have a very strong influence on man's fate hence its movement is important. Rahu (8) and Ketu (9) are unique to Asian astrology and will be explained later.

The planet table for birth chart has 9 columns.

The first column lists the number representing the planets.

The second column lists the name of the planets as well as the Lagna, denoted by the letter L.

The third column lists the number representing the zodiac signs.

The fourth column lists the name of the zodiac signs.

The fifth column lists the exact location of the planets in each zodiac sign in degrees (each sign comprising 30 degrees).

The sixth column lists the exact location of the planets in each zodiac sign in minutes, (one degree comprising 60 minutes).

The seventh column indicates whether any planet is in unusual movement; retrograde (backward) movement is denoted by the letter *R*, unusually slow movement denoted by the letter *S*, and unusually fast movement denoted by the letter *F*.

The eighth column lists the Nawang. The first number is the number of the Nawang (there are 9 Nawangs in each zodiac sign), and the second number indicates the planet that is the Ruler of that Nawang.

The ninth column indicates whether Lagna or any planet is a Nawang Exaltation, denoted by the letter *E*.

Planets in transit

Your birth chart is the snapshot photo of the position of the planets in the sky at the moment of your birth. Your habits and behavior, hence, your personality, is very much influenced by the position of the planets at the moment of your birth. Your habits and behavior, in turn, tend to influence your future achievements and your reactions to the world. Based on statistics, astrology can, therefore, predict the likely course of your future.

The planets, of course, move on after your birth. The position of the planets after your birth is called planets in transit. The position of the planets in transit varies every millisecond. Their positions also influence your thinking and events. For the purpose of illustration, the position of the planets in the chart of Princess Diana, both at birth and one year after birth, are shown here.

The birth chart of Princess Diana

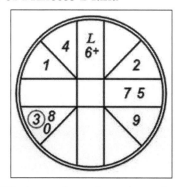

Thai astrology date: Saturday
Calendar Sunday 2 July 1961 at 01.45

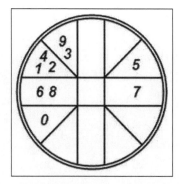

Chart of planets in transit on 2 July 1962

You will see in the chart at the end of one year after Diana's birth that the planets have moved. The Sun (1), even though in Gemini in both charts, has in fact gone round all the zodiac signs and ended up in the same sign. All planets including the Sun (1) and the Moon (2) move in counterclockwise direction, except Rahu (8) and Ketu (9) which move in clockwise direction. Each planet moves at different speeds. Both types of chart can be generated from our website.

2. The Position of the Planets

How does one determine the position of the planets?

Since ancient times, astrologers determine the position of the planets by marking them against some fixed points in the sky. The fixed points are star constellations that are extremely far away, beyond the solar system. These star constellations, which in relation to earth are always fixed in the sky, are compared to earthly objects. They represent the zodiac signs.

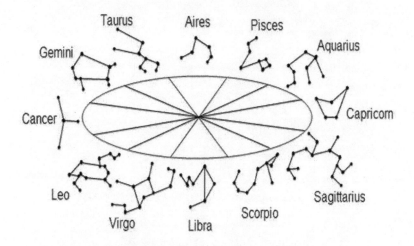

View of the star constellations used to locate the zodiac signs as seen from earth

The birth chart in Thai astrology is the form of a circle. The circle is actually the sky as viewed from earth. The sky is divided into 12 sections, one for each zodiac sign. Each sign is divided into 30 degrees, each degree divided into 60 minutes. The description of the position of Jupiter can be at 14 degrees and 10 minutes in the sign of Capricorn, in the example of Diana's birth chart.

2. The Position of the Planets

The zodiac signs *(Rasi)*

In the Thai astrological diary, the Zodiac signs are similar to modern astrology, but are also listed by number for convenient reference as follow;

The Shape of Earthly objects	Zodiac Sign	Thai numbering
Ram	Aries	0
Bull	Taurus	1
Twins	Gemini	2
Crab	Cancer	3
Lion	Leo	4
Virgin	Virgo	5
Balancing scale	Libra	6
Scorpion	Scorpio	7
Shooting arrow	Sagittarius	8
Water snake	Capricorn	9
Water bottle	Aquarius	10
Fish	Pisces	11

 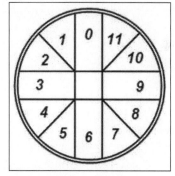

Zodiac signs and the numbering system used in the Thai diary

How the signs are grouped

The zodiac signs are grouped. This grouping is very important for Thai astrology because statistics have shown that signs in the same group have some significant similar characteristics which will be discussed in details later. The grouping is as follow;

Quadruped *(Passava)* which are the three signs of four-legged animals: Aries (ram), Taurus (bull), Leo (lion)

Human *(Nara)* which are the four signs of human form or human utensils: Gemini (twins), Virgo (virgin), Libra (balancing scale), Sagittarius (shooting arrow), Aquarius (water bottle)

Aquatic *(Umpuj)* which are the three signs of marine animals: Cancer (crab), Capricorn (water snake), Pisces (fish)

Scorpion *(Keta)* which is the only sign of insect: Scorpio (scorpion)

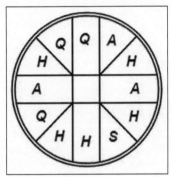

Q – Quadruped, H – Human, A – Aquatic, S – Scorpio

The four elements

Signs are grouped into four elements: fire, wind, earth and water. Signs of the same element form a perfect triangle in the birth chart as shown.

Fire element signs are Aries, Leo and Sagittarius. In the Thai chart they form a triangle pointing upward. Aries is the mother of Fire signs.

Wind element signs are Libra, Aquarius and Gemini, forming a triangle pointing downward. Libra is the mother of Wind signs.

Earth element signs are Capricorn, Taurus and Virgo, forming a triangle pointing to the right. Capricorn is the mother of Earth signs.

Water element signs are Cancer, Scorpio and Pisces, forming a triangle pointing to the left. Cancer is the mother of Water signs.

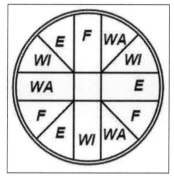

F – fire, WI – wind, E – earth, WA – water

What is Lagna?

Lagna (denoted by the letter L in the birth chart) is the point on the birth chart that reflects your particular self. It is the point at which sun ray first touches the earth in the easternmost direction at the time that you were born. Imagine the sun ray touching the earth along the equator. At sunrise each day, the person born in the geographical location that the sun ray first touches the earth in the easternmost direction will have his/her Lagna in the same zodiac sign with the sun. The point on the circumference of the equator, at which the sun ray first touches the earth in the easternmost direction, is always the same. However, the earth will gradually turn each region along the equator, in turn, to first touch the sun ray as it rotates. The easternmost point of the earth is always the Lagna no matter how much the earth has turned.

Scientifically, therefore, Lagna of every person should be at the same spot on the birth chart, and the rotation of the earth causes the whole birth chart, along with the position of the planets, to slowly rotate. This is the way it is presented in Western astrology. However, in Thai astrology presentation, the birth charts, as well as the transit charts, are instead fixed with

Aries always on top, with Lagna of each person rotating instead. This makes the charts simpler.

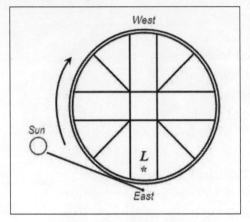

Birth time at sun rise

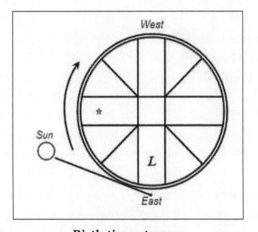

Birth time at noon
*denotes the geographical location of the person's birth.
The position of Lagna is always the point at which the sun ray first touches the earth in the easternmost direction no matter how much the earth has rotated.

In Thai astrology there are two schools of thought about how to treat the time of birth for people born outside Thailand. This results in different placements of Lagna.

The first school believes that planet positions are the same the world over; therefore, it recommends using your local time in placing the Lagna, because it relates to the local time of sunrise. This method treats the person as if he/she is born in Thailand, with some minor adjustment done to take into account the latitude and the longitude of the locality.

The second school believes that while the local time of sunrise is important, it requires statistics to be collected in that locality. Thai astrology is based on records gathered from observations made in Thailand; therefore, foreign local time should be converted back to Thai time.

We subscribe to the second school. Therefore, when converted to Thai time, the position of Lagna relative to the sun, as described above, applies only to Thai time. We confirmed that the second method is more useful by testing many birth charts of celebrities born around the world, especially in relation to the first (Self) House in transit, which will be explained later. However, if you want to produce your birth chart based on the first school, you can simply put in your local time and specify GMT+07.00. The program will construct a birth chart as if you were born in Thailand at that time.

3. Princess Diana's Birth Chart

Princess Diana's planets

You can see from Princess Diana's birth chart that her Lagna is in Aries while her Sun (represented by no. 1) is in Gemini, indicating her time of birth adjusted to Thai system to be a few hours after midnight.

For Diana therefore, her planet positions are as follow:

Lagna is in Aries. The Sun (1) is in Gemini. The Moon (2) is in Aquarius. Mars (3) is in Leo. Mercury (4) is in Taurus. Jupiter (5) is in Capricorn. Venus (6) is in Aries. Saturn (7) is in Capricorn. Rahu (8) is in Leo. Ketu (9) is in Sagittarius. Uranus (0) is in Leo.

How should Princess Diana have read her daily horoscopes in newspapers?

Daily horoscopes in newspapers are done for people with the same Sun (1) sign. Diana's Sun (1) is in Gemini; therefore, she should read the horoscope for Gemini people. The Sun (1) is so important in a birth chart that even without the exact birth time, one can still read a lot of information from the position of other planets in relation to the Sun (1). This is why some general predictions in daily horoscopes can be made for all the people with the Sun (1) in the same sign.

However, please note that the movement of the sun in the Thai astrological diary is based on the Hindu *Suriya Siddhanta* almanac and not the weather seasons (Tropical zodiac) as in Western astrology. In the Thai astrological diary, the sun moves from one sign to the next between the 14-16th day of each month compared to the 21-23rd day in Western astrology. Therefore, do not use the Thai diary to determine which sun sign in Western horoscopes for you to follow.

What if two people are born at exactly the same time in exactly the same location?

Thai astrology believes that two people born at exactly the same time in exactly the same location will have more or less the same life, similar habits and behavior, similar outlook towards life events and towards other people, similar interests and aspirations. Major life events that happen to them will also be the same. The only difference will be their levels of achievement and their lasting impact on the world. The person born to the family with more prominence and higher economic and social stature, basically starting from a higher ground, will naturally end up higher.

The same amount of money may be considered by one person as large and significant, but by another as just ordinary. Also, a person that is a leader of a small country cannot have as much impact as another with the same birth chart that leads a large country.

Part II:

Matters Related to Life are Reflected

in the Houses

4. The Houses in the Birth Chart *(Phob)*

Each Zodiac sign in the birth chart represents a House. Each House relates to certain matter in the person's life. All Houses have one or more planet as its Ruler. Life events are influenced by the planets that occupy that House as well as by the planet that is the Ruler of that House, both at the time of birth and later when they transit into that House. All birth charts have twelve Houses, similar to the number of Zodiac signs. In Thai astrology, the first House is the one where Lagna (denoted by the letter L) resides. Counting the Houses always goes counterclockwise, with the House in which Lagna occupies being counted as the first House.

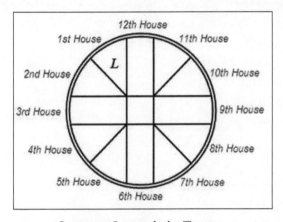

Suppose Lagna is in Taurus.
House numbers start with Lagna as number 1
then go counterclockwise

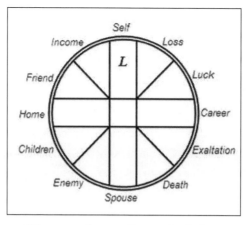

Here we change Lagna to Aries.

**The twelve Houses of the birth chart
are shown above**

The name of the Houses is as follow:

First House	Self *(Tanu)*
Second House	Income *(Gadoompa)*
Third House	Friend *(Sahajja)*
Fourth House	Home *(Bhandu)*
Fifth House	Children *(Putta)*
Sixth House	Enemy *(Ahri)*
Seventh House	Spouse *(Pattani)*
Eighth House	Death *(Morana)*
Ninth House	Exaltation *(Supa)*
Tenth House	Career *(Karma)*
Eleventh House	Luck *(Lapa)*
Twelfth House	Loss *(Vinasana)*

The First House – Self

This is the most important House. In Thai language, it is called *Tanu*, translated as Self. This House is about yourself, your place of birth, your disposition, your body constitution, your physical and mental strength and weakness. It is also about your overall

21

behavior, your appearance and your health. All these traits directly affect your personality and your outlook to life. Therefore, it is the most important foundation to predict the probability of eventual success in all other matters.

The Second House – Income

This House is about your earning capacity, your ability to accumulate wealth and assets, business success, generosity and your outlook towards savings and spending. It is also about inheritance. The planet is this house is termed the Leading Engine because it directly leads Lagna. The Leading Engine, the quality and characteristic of that planet, will therefore have a very strong influence on your life.

Leading Engine *(Soonpaha)*

Each planet that acts as the Leading Engine gives different tendencies to the person's life as follows:

The Sun (1) will make the person ambitious; strive to achieve high position especially in governmental or administrative work, as well as successful in wealth accumulation.

The Moon (2) will make him/her good at human relationship not only in family life, but also in work.

Mars (3) will make the person a strong leader of organization or any work that requires courage and strong conviction.

Mercury (4) will make the person well versed in worldly knowledge, and sensible in commercial activities.

Jupiter (5) will make the person interested in academic or intellectual pursuit as well as in developing sound judgment.

Venus (6) will make the person good at relationship with family and friends, a popular person.

Saturn (7) will make the person poised and pensive, good at dealing with elders and people with authority.

Rahu (8) will make the person aggressive and big hearted, able to attract followers but, at the same time, there is a risk of overspending especially if Rahu (8) is the Ruler of the sixth (Enemy) House.

When there is more than one planet in the second (Income) House, the Leading Engine is the planet that is in the strongest position (in descending order – Ruler, Exalted, Perseverance, Assistance).

The Third House – Friend

This House is about your brothers, your sisters, friends, close associates, neighbors, work colleagues and agents, social mingling and social circle. It is also about correspondences, which are mostly done between friends and associates. It is also about short journeys, which are normally done to communicate with friends and associates.

The Fourth House – Home

This House is about things that come with your birth. It is about your relatives, your father's and mother's clans, taking care of others, your own residential abode, the possession of land and real estate as well as vehicles. In a man's chart, it is also about his mother, and in a woman's chart, her father.

The Fifth House – Children

This House is about your children (or the lack of), their life achievements, young servants and subordinates. It is also about teaching small children, social entertainment, enjoyment and pleasure, puppy love, craving for things, collecting things and pets. It can indicate carelessness, lack of seriousness and careless spending on non-essentials like a teenager. It is also about things related to young associates, new lovers other than the main spouse, and sudden luck, especially promotion and money from gambling or speculation.

The Sixth House – Enemy

This is the first of the three Malefic *(Dusthana)* Houses. It is about enemies, opponents, bad intention and plots being hatched against you, as well as accidents and illness, servants, cousins, expenses, incurring debts, law suits and defeat caused by adversaries.

The Seventh House – Spouse

This is about your marriage, your spouse or life partner, business partners or counterparties in a contract, the opposite party in a law suit, the open enemy, as well as temporary places of dwelling, hotels.

The Eighth House – Death

This is the second of the three Malefic Houses. It is about death, opposition, failure, disappointment, destruction, illness and hospitalization, things related to death, such as inheritance, will, heirloom, or luck from unexpected sources, especially foreign, as well as money recovered from debtors long written off. It can also mean a change of job, relocation, long distance travel not associated with happiness, settlement abroad far away, and foreigners.

The Ninth House – Exaltation

This House is about progress, receiving assistance from people of authority or people in a higher position that can help you to achieve your goals, attaining exalted position, upgrading, promotion in career and academic success, as well as religious belief or holy undertaking, goodness and integrity. In a man's chart, it is about his father. In a woman's chart, it is about her mother. It is also about long distance travel associated with happiness and foreign dealings. This is the House that reflects happiness and harmony in your own family.

The Tenth House – Career

This House is about career, the progress and support that you get for the advancement of your career. It is also about heavy burden and responsibility, and administrative work. While the ninth (Exaltation) House reflects the high position that you attain, the tenth (Career) House reflects the nature and content of work involved. In the man's chart, this House should be read together with the ninth (Exaltation) House about his father. In the woman's chart, it should be read together with the fourth (Home) House about her father.

The Eleventh House – Luck

This House is about addition, augmentation, luck, successful conclusion, and money earned from lucky circumstances, support and assistance from friends, advisers and other people, political support from electorates.

The Twelfth House – Loss

This is the third of the three Malefic Houses. It is about sudden losses, double crossing, murder; a loner that prefers his/her own company to social mingling; separation, settlement abroad, calamity, law suits, imprisonment or detention, and things happening secretly, suddenly or unexpectedly. It is also about money received in secret, plots behind the scene, traitors that are close to the person, close servants, secret lovers, and excessive spending or bankruptcy.

5. The Planets

Sun for honor and position

Moon for attraction and charm

Mars for courage and resiliency

Mercury for diplomacy and speech

Jupiter for intelligence and being righteous

Venus for being sensuous and wealth

Saturn for hardship and long wait

Rahu for senseless addiction

Ketu for longevity

Uranus for accident and calamity

Each planet has the ability to influence man in its unique way, according to its position in relation to Lagna and to other planets, both at birth and later when the planets move in transit daily. Each can influence man to take up habits and behavior that reflect its quality, both good and bad.

The Sun (1)

Ruler:	**Leo**
Insecure:	**Aquarius**
Exalted:	**Aries**
Fall:	**Libra**
Perseverance:	**Cancer**
Assistance:	**Gemini**
Transit time	
Through each sign:	**About 30 days**
12 zodiac signs:	**1 year**

Thai astrology believes the birth chart of the earth itself (imagining the earth to be a person) to have Lagna in Aries. Therefore, Leo is the fifth (Children) House of the earth which is related to children and birth. Because the sun is a necessary condition for the creation of most lives, it is appropriate to be the Ruler of Leo.

The Sun (1) is the shining light to all forms of life. It is the main foundation. With the Sun (1) in a good position in the birth chart, the person will be of a bright and sunny disposition. It gives him/her ambitions, a strong mind, pride, steadfastness, willingness to take calculated risks, and the ability to lead and make decisions. He/she is prepared to make sacrifices for higher achievement in life and for honor. He/she is prepared to volunteer, to try to help out, to take the chance to show his/her skills. It also gives the person a taste for luxurious things and the habit of showing off possessions.

With the Sun (1) in a strong position, the person is good at academics, farsighted, willing to explore new ideas and possess good administrative ability. He/she is well poised, agile and prefers to be unrestricted, pushing Him/herself to be a leader. The Sun (1) in a bad position makes the person less prepared to make sacrifices, less willing to push on, indecisive and avoid taking risks. He/she is impatient and can do things in too much of a rush without due care. His/her mood can be changeable. He/she can get mad but also get over it easily. He/she relies too much on hearsay and rumors, being narrow-minded, feeling inadequate, boastful, conceited and too easy with his/her money. He/she has an inability to lead and take responsibility.

The Sun (1) also represents father. In a strong position, it indicates a father of high society or a high ranking position. A poor Sun (1) may indicate a separation from the father at an early age. In a woman's birth chart, the Sun (1) also represents her husband.

The Moon (2)

Ruler:	Cancer
Insecure:	Capricorn
Exalted:	Taurus
Fall:	Scorpio
Perseverance:	Aries
Assistance:	Virgo
Transit time	
Through each sign:	About 2 ½ days
12 zodiac signs:	About 27 days

In the earth's chart, Cancer is the fourth (Home) House which is about family. The moon represents motherhood, hence is appropriate to be Ruler of this House.

The Moon (2) is the shining light at night with a softer tone. It is about enjoyment, kindness, emotions, sweet manner, and physical attraction. In a woman's birth chart, the Moon (2), in a strong position, makes her especially attractive. If it is reachable by Mars (3), the planet that gives the person courage and dare, it can make the person overly active in romance. If the Moon (2) is too strong on a man's chart, it can make him soft hearted, acting feminine, and preferring to follow rather than lead. The Moon (2) in a man's chart also represents his wife.

With the Moon (2) in a good position, the person is mellow, sensitive, dreamy and calm. He/she has good manner, interested in beauty and charm. He/she is able to attract assistance from family and friends. His/her hallmark is a practical approach to life and work. He/she is gentle, detail driven, has good taste, taking good care of his/her own family, and careful of money. Career directly related to the Moon (2) includes cooking, nursing and water related products.

The Moon (2) in a bad position can make the person uninterested in charm and manner. His /her feelings are too easily hurt. His/her mood can be changeable, sulky, digging into too much detail.

When you analyze the planets in transit, you would normally use the Moon (2) as the Ruler of Cancer. However, because the transit time of the moon is so rapid, Thai astrology looks also at Saturn (7) in transit as another Ruler of Cancer.

Mars (3)

Ruler:	**Aries and Scorpio**
Insecure:	**Libra and Taurus**
Exalted:	**Capricorn**
Fall:	**Cancer**
Perseverance:	**Virgo**
Assistance:	**Taurus**
Transit time	
Through each sign:	**About 45 days at normal speed**
12 zodiac signs:	**About 1 ½ years**

In the earth's chart, Aries is the first (Self) House, while Scorpio is the eighth (Death) House. The former represents life and the latter the end of life. Mars is the planet of energy which is the essence of life, therefore it is appropriate to be the Ruler of both Houses.

Mars (3) is comfortable in the situation of war and conflicts. It gives the person strength, courage, love of adventure, endurance, energy, speed and stubbornness. With Mars (3) in a good position, the person is energetic, hard working, prepared to take risks even with his/her life, and make sacrifices. He/she is quick to react, open and responsible, big hearted. One can easily trust the person with a strong Mars (3) to carry out promises and deliver work on time, regardless of difficulty. He/she excels in military, police, weaponry, sports or work related to machine tools, electrical or engineering operation.

Mars (3) in a bad position makes the person lack energy, courage, or it can be the opposite and make the person too rash, physically or verbally abusive and accident prone, especially accidents related to machinery. He/she can also become angry too easily. His/her technical ability with machine tools is low.

Mercury (4)

Ruler:	**Gemini and Virgo**
Insecure:	**Sagittarius and Pisces**
Exalted:	**Virgo**
Fall:	**Pisces**
Perseverance:	**Leo**
Assistance:	**Leo**
Transit time	
Through each sign:	**About 28 days at normal speed**
12 zodiac signs:	**About 1 year**

In the earth's chart, Gemini is the third (Friend) House, while Virgo is the sixth (Enemy) House. The former represents our needs to have siblings and close friends, but the relationship, if not well managed, will make them end up in the latter House as enemies. Mercury is the planet of communication skill, which is the basis of all relationship, therefore is appropriate to be the Ruler of both Houses.

Mercury (4) is the planet of thoughts, speech, negotiations, plots and plans, commerce and trade, any activity that benefits from negotiation, advertising and promotion, but it can err on the side of easy panic and wavering judgment as well as uncertainty, adaptability and being easily bored. With Mercury (4) in a good position, the person is a good speaker, witty, able to build and maintain good professional relationship. He/she is good at diplomacy, correspondence, teaching, mathematics, language, writing books and plays as well as education. He/she has a good memory, is resourceful, a master of strategies, easy to assimilate and digest new information, and easily absorbs the general type of knowledge. Careers related to Mercury (4) are accounting, secretary, writer, diplomat, law and acting. Leaders need to have strong Mercury (4) to enable them to communicate and persuade through speech.

Mercury (4) in a bad position can make the person speak out too freely without tact or without substance, and with poor memory and poor knowledge of commerce. He/she may also tell lies and make up stories, resort to forgeries, and be too easy to change his/her mind. He/she tends to struggle with new information, and has low absorption capacity. His/her morality can also be low, relying more on duplicity and lame excuses.

Jupiter (5)	
Ruler:	Sagittarius and Pisces
Insecure:	Gemini and Virgo
Exalted:	Cancer
Fall:	Capricorn
Perseverance:	Scorpio
Assistance:	Aries
Transit time	
Through each sign:	About 1 year at normal speed
12 zodiac signs:	About 12 years

In the earth's chart, Sagittarius is the ninth (Exaltation) House, while Pisces is the twelfth (Loss) House. The former represents honor, glory and permanency. The latter represents the risk of its decline and disappearance. Jupiter is the planet of intelligence which is the most important ingredient for honor or for losing it, therefore is appropriate to be the Ruler of both Houses.

Jupiter (5) is the planet of high morale, kindness, protection, patronage, success, fairness, wealth and plenty, study, willingness to teach, respect, good, thorough and balanced judgment and intellectual capacity. With Jupiter (5) in a good position, the person is interested in education and intellectual pursuit. Intelligence of Jupiter (5) is the academic, non trivial type, as opposed to the street smart mercantile type of Mercury (4). He/she values honesty, gratitude and justice, preferring the company of scholars and thinkers. He/she excels in all types of administrative work, judiciary work, university, banking, medicine and government, looking after other people. He/she is good at putting him/herself in other's point of view; an optimist at heart.

Jupiter (5) in a bad position will tend to make the person lack good judgment and struggle in education. He/she is ungrateful, insincere, and unable to hold on to money. He/she can be full of tricks, relying on procrastination and showing off. He/she can be a non-believer in religion, someone who thinks too highly of themselves, deceiving him/herself in the process.

Venus (6)

Ruler:	**Taurus and Libra**
Insecure:	**Scorpio and Aries**
Exalted:	**Pisces**
Fall:	**Virgo**
Perseverance:	**Sagittarius**
Assistance:	**Cancer**
Transit time	
Through each sign:	**About 28 days at normal speed**
12 zodiac signs:	**About 1 year**

In the earth's chart, Taurus is the second (Income) House, while Libra is the seventh (Spouse) House. They represent man's desire for comfort and enjoyment which comes from having both money and spouse. Venus is the planet that is, on the one hand, associated with love, yearning, beauty, physical arousal, sexual appeal, good company, and, on the other hand, associated with money and wealth, therefore is appropriate to be the Ruler of both Houses.

With Venus (6) in a good position, the person gives high

importance to his/her physical desires, hence increasing his/her chance of a successful marriage (especially when Venus (6) is in Libra). It also makes him/her successful in earning money and wealth (especially when Venus (6) is in Taurus). He/she may excel in banking, commerce, or public services, as well as acting and drama. He/she has a happy disposition, is well groomed, and enjoys social activities. He/she is the person of society, with a kind heart, someone who appreciates art and beautiful things. He/she values love highly. Venus (6) is the career of economics, financial, fiscal, liberal arts, fine art, acting, music, beauty products, restaurants, garments, jewelry, and social work.

Venus (6) in a bad position can give the person disappointment in love, or in earning and wealth, tending to be short all the time. He/she may lack social skills, tending to boast and bluff his/her way through life. He/she can be unhappy in marriage, disappointed in love because of either sexual excess or sexual deficiency.

Saturn (7)

Ruler:	**Capricorn and Co-Ruler of Aquarius**
Insecure:	**Cancer and Leo**
Exalted:	**Libra**
Fall:	**Aries**
Perseverance:	**Taurus**
Assistance:	**Scorpio**
Transit time	
Through each sign:	**About 2 ½ years at normal speed**
12 zodiac signs:	**About 30 years**

In the earth's chart, Capricorn is the tenth (Career) House. Work requires physical toil and endurance, which is appropriate for the nature of Saturn to be its Ruler.

Saturn (7) is the planet of delay, tenseness, frugality, deliberation, worry, separation, heavy burden, suffering and prolonged illness. It also gives morbidity, lunacy, deep reflection, poor intelligence, and envy. He/she is very methodical and will tend to absorb too much of the surrounding events for his/her own reflection. He/she will not easily trust others, always looking for interior motives. He/she tends to be conservative and prepared to follow past customs and practices. No matter how successful in career or how well off in finance, he/she does not feel comfortable with life, often feeling that he/she bears a heavy burden. With Saturn (7) in a good position, the person is good at biding his/her time, waiting and trying various things, thorough in work. He/she can be an architect, an inventor, or an artist, the type who is prepared to go through multiple failures before the eventual success. Saturn (7) can also relate to construction, industrial production, activities related to labor or to farm.

However, if it is in a bad position, it can make the person overly suspicious, morbid, a loner, too self centered, relying only on his/her own point of view and stubborn. He/she can be selfish, unkind, someone with a black heart that can in extreme cases consider committing crime. He/she can also be physically handicapped, greedy, devious, a pessimist at heart.

Rahu (8)

Ruler:	**Co-Ruler of Aquarius**
Insecure:	**Leo**
Exalted:	**Scorpio**
Fall:	**Taurus**
Perseverance:	**Capricorn**
Assistance:	**Libra**
Transit time	
Through each sign:	**1 ½ years**
12 zodiac signs:	**18 years**

In the earth's chart, Aquarius is the eleventh (Luck) House. Luck requires us to take chances where necessary. Rahu is the planet of gambling and taking chances, and therefore is appropriate to be the Ruler of this House.

Rahu (8) shares Rulership of Aquarius with both Saturn (7) and Uranus (0). When one examines the House that is situated in Aquarius, one has to look at all three planets. Read with Rahu (8) first, then re-examine with Saturn (7) and make the final check with Uranus (0). Rahu (8) is like an ill gusty wind that can blow and destroy things. It can lead the person to be a gang leader, the godfather. It can fill him/her with intoxication, careless wavering and improper judgment. He/she can be swayed by rumors and sweet words, too easily addicted to sex or gambling. It also represents a loud mouth, improper manner, going over limits, over confidence, power maniac, holding too high opinion about self, as well as obscurity.

With Rahu (8) in a good position, the person has a big heart, enjoys taking risks, winning at most gambles and easily attracting the following of people around him/her. He/she can be secretive, full of tactical and crafty plans but may, at times, present him/herself as being less able. He/she is a fighter and tends to be good at police work, or in gathering intelligence or underground information. Many people in political positions have strong Rahu (8) in their birth charts. However good the position, it still makes the person somewhat greedy. Rahu (8) in a bad position will tend to deprive him/her of good judgment. He/she may be prepared to use his/her position for improper personal gains. He/she can be attracted to too much gambling, intoxication, lower class people and gangsters. He/she can be gullible, easily parting with wealth or inheritance.

The careers related to Rahu (8) also include law, customs, tobacco and alcohol related products. Rahu (8) is also the planet of change, especially for planets in transit. This occurs both when a planet in transit is in conjunction with Rahu (8) in the birth chart, and when Rahu (8) in transit is in conjunction with a planet in the birth chart.

Ketu (9)

Ruler:	None
Transit time	
Through each sign:	2 months
12 zodiac signs:	2 years

Ketu (9) has no Rulership, but it is considered to be in a strong position if it is in any one of the four zodiac signs that do not have any planet in Exalted position. The signs are Gemini, Leo, Sagittarius and Aquarius. Ketu (9) represents the soul and spirit. It enhances both the good and the bad quality of other planets. It is like a long river, therefore it symbolizes longevity, antiquity, history and inheritance, having sixth sense as well as things foreign, sacred subjects and religion, exaltation, king and royalty, and attaining high honorable positions.

With Ketu (9) in a good position, the person tends to be successful in his/her career as well as have a long life. He/she is quick minded, intelligent, farsighted, resourceful and creative. His/her success can be linked to dealing with foreigners or elders. Ketu (9) in a bad position tends to make the person too secretive, full of deceiving plans, selfish and untruthful. He/she can be like a fox, too clever for his/her own good, without scruples and too immersed in spiritual occult activities. It can also indicate the person of self illusion, or deranged mind especially if it is in conjunction with Saturn (7) in the birth chart.

Uranus (0)

Ruler:	Co-Ruler of Aquarius
Transit time	
Through each sign:	About 7 years at normal speed
12 zodiac signs:	About 84 years

Uranus (0) is a co-Ruler of Aquarius. It represents emptiness. It is a black hole into which good things can be involuntarily absorbed. It denotes separation, death, accidents, destruction, mystery, haunting experiences and sudden calamity.

With Uranus (0) in a good position, the person can avoid unusually bad sudden illness or fatal accidents. This planet is also about coup and revolution, sudden disruption to the established order. Therefore, it can make the person innovative with changes. He/she can think outside the box, ready to introduce new things, new technology, fond of scientific experiments. With Uranus (0) in a bad position, the person runs a high risk of accident and severe, permanent illness. He/she may be too self centered, self opinionated, secretive, under current, disrespectful of authority, a rebel and willing to destroy the established orders. He/she can be cold hearted.

Other planets discovered in the past two hundred years

Thai astrology has not yet accumulated enough statistics regarding the new planets that were discovered in the past two hundred years, which are Neptune and Pluto. They are not visible to the naked eyes, so their statistics cannot go back very far.

Also, because they are at the outer perimeters from the sun, their transit time through the twelve zodiac signs are extremely long, as indicated by their orbit time around the solar system: 165 years for Neptune and 248 years for Pluto. These new planets are therefore not very useful in predicting events year to year. Being at the outer perimeters, their influences can also weaken when they transit through certain sections of their elliptical paths that are too far from the sun and the earth. For example, Thai astrology, as quoted by Mr. Thep Sarigbutr in one of his books, considers Pluto in the last century to be near enough to have any influence only between 1900 and 1952. After 1952, it was too far away to have any influence until it comes within the vicinity again from around 2011 onward.

Beneficent planets and Maleficent planets *(Supakroah and Bapakroah)*

The Moon (2), Mercury (4), Jupiter (5) and Venus (6) are called Beneficent planets. If these planets are Rulers of the Benefic Houses, they will tend to give their good quality to the person. The good quality will accrue and accumulate gently over time as the person matures. They tend to make the person's life well adjusted, his/her development continuous. Benefic Houses are the Houses related to good matter of life, which are all the Houses except the Malefic Houses (the sixth (Enemy) House, the eighth (Death) House and the eleventh (Loss) House).

If the Beneficent planets are Rulers of the Malefic Houses, they will give their bad quality to the person. The bad quality will also develop gently over time, and tends to be less than the damage from the Maleficent planets. It is as if one may have the ability to arrest the development and shed the bad habits and behavior, if one really wants to.

Mars (3), Saturn (7), Rahu (8) and Uranus (0) are termed the Maleficent planets. If they are Rulers of the Benefic Houses, they can give the person their good quality also. But the good quality will come in a rush, almost unexpectedly.

On the other hand, if the Maleficent planets are Rulers of the Malefic Houses, they will tend to give their bad quality in a quick manner, like a tempest.

The Sun (1) and Ketu (9) are Neutral planets. They add their power to whichever planet they have aspect with. The examples of the birth charts below are where Saturn (7) and Rahu (8) can give the person their good quality despite their being Maleficent planets:

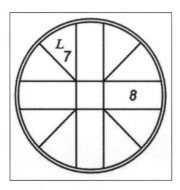

Birth chart A

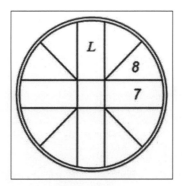

Birth chart B

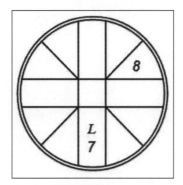

Birth chart C

In birth chart A, Saturn (7) is the Ruler of the ninth (Exaltation) House. It is in conjunction with Lagna. Having exaltation in the House of self gives the tendency for achievement and honor. The good quality of Saturn (7) is further enhanced by Rahu (8). Rahu (8)'s enhancement occurs because it is the Friendly Pair of Saturn (7), and it is in Capricorn which is the Ruler House of Saturn (7), therefore its influence is automatically transmitted to Saturn (7). Rahu (8) is also in trine with Saturn (7).

In birth chart B, Saturn (7) is the Ruler of the tenth (Career) House and is in its own House therefore it is strong. Having a strong planet in the House of career gives the tendency for success and permanency in career. The good quality of Saturn (7) is also enhanced by Rahu (8). Rahu (8)'s enhancement occurs because it is in its own House, thus makes it strong. Rahu (8) is also in the House where Saturn (7) is the co-Ruler; therefore its influence is automatically transmitted to Saturn (7).

In birth chart C, Saturn (7) is the Ruler of the fourth (Home) House. It is in conjunction with Lagna. Saturn (7) is in Exalted position, therefore it is especially strong. Having the Ruler of the House related to assets in the House of self indicates success in accumulating wealth and properties. Again, this example shows how Rahu (8) can enhance the good quality of Saturn (7). Rahu (8) is in Aquarius, the fifth (Children) House. It is in its own House, therefore it is strong. Having the Ruler of the House that is related to sudden luck in a strong position makes the person lucky in speculation. Rahu (8)'s influence is also automatically transmitted to Saturn (7) through it being in the House with Saturn (7) as the co-Ruler, as well as its position in trine with Saturn (7).

Unusual movement of the planets

Unusual movement of the planet can occur in three ways: retrograde *(Puktr)* denoted by the letter *R*, unusually fast

(Serd) denoted by the letter *F*, and unusually slow *(Mont)* denoted by the letter *S*. Retrograde movement is when the planet moves in a backward direction. The birth chart is like a snapshot of the positions of the planets at the time of birth. Therefore, the birth chart itself cannot capture the retrograde movement. Instead, the indication is given in the planet table. Unusually fast and slow refer to the speed that is abnormal and faster or slower than usual.

All planets can have periods of unusual movement, except the Sun (1), the Moon (2), Rahu (8) and Ketu (9). Retrograde planets do not actually move backward. They simply appear to do so when we look at them from the earth. This is caused by the different orbit speeds and relative positions of the planets to the earth.

The effects of planets in unusual movement are as follow:

A. If the planet is the Ruler of a Benefic House, or if the planet is situated in a Benefic House, and its movement is –
Unusually fast, it would give its good quality to the person.
Unusually slow, it would still give its good quality but less than it would at normal speed.
Retrograde, it would instead give its bad quality.

B. If the planet is the Ruler of a Malefic House, or if the planet resides in a Malefic House, and its movement is –
Unusually fast, it would give its bad quality.
Unusually slow, it would still give its bad quality but less than it would at normal speed.
Retrograde, it would instead give its good quality.
Also when a planet is too close to the Sun (1), within 3 degrees of each other, it would lose its good quality, being overwhelmed by the Sun (1). If it happens to Mercury (4), for example, the person tends to be poor in correspondence and speech. But in this situation, if

41

Mercury (4) is in unusual movement, its good quality is not only unaffected, but instead enhanced, as in Barrack Obama's case.

6. The Power of the Planets

The strength of the planets

Each planet exhibits different levels of strength depending on its position in the zodiac signs. Explanations for this phenomenon are related to the brightness level when the planets transit into each sign.

You will see that Mars (3) and Mercury (4) have two positions even when in the very same zodiac sign. That planet should be read to have both types of the quality associated with such positions.

Ruler positions and Insecure positions *(Kaset and Pra)*

The planet that is Ruler of a particular sign appears bright when it transits into that sign. The brightness level is just right, not too glaring, signifying endurance. For example, this happens when the Sun (1) is in Leo during the summer season, making its astrological quality long lasting and secured.

On the other hand, when it transits through the sign directly opposite, for example the Sun (1) in Aquarius, during the winter season appears least bright. The Sun (1) here is called Insecure, meaning its astrological quality is absent or insecure. The planet in Insecure positions is either unable to deliver its good quality, or delivers it with uncertainty, or after a long struggle, a long wait. You have to memorize the position of the Ruler planets. All astrological analysis will refer to this information.

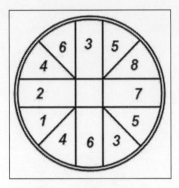

Planets in Ruler positions

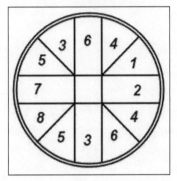

Planets in Insecure positions

Ruler positions divide the signs in a birth chart into two parts, day and night. Day signs start from Leo and go counterclockwise to end at Capricorn. The Rulers are positioned in each sign according to their distance from the solar system center as follow:

Sun (1) – Mercury (4) – Venus (6) – Mars (3) – Jupiter (5) – Saturn (7)

Night signs start from Cancer and go clockwise to end at Aquarius. The Rulers are also positioned in each sign according to their distance from the sun, but with the Moon (2) serving as the starting point and with Rahu (8) replacing Saturn (7).

The quality of Ruler positions and Insecure positions

If a person's birth chart has a planet in Ruler position, his/her habits and character, hence his/her future life would tend to be secure in whichever matter related to the House of which that planet is the Ruler and the House that the planet occupies.

With the Sun (1) as the Ruler in its own House, he/she concentrates on attaining high education, obtaining skills to help him/her in achieving career goal.

With the Moon (2) as the Ruler in its own House, he/she concentrates on social relationship, using the skills to help in obtaining assistance and support from others.

With Mars (3) as the Ruler in its own House, he/she is courageous, rebellious, enduring and hard working, making him/her successful in his/her achievements.

With Mercury (4) as the Ruler in its own House, he/she has verbal skills, the ability to negotiate and persuade, which will help in obtaining assistance and support from others.

With Jupiter (5) as the Ruler in its own House, he/she emphasizes education and doing the right things, which will help in achievements.

With Venus (6) as the Ruler in its own House, he/she concentrates on money management skills, a comfortable life, and amorous relationship, which will help in obtaining assistance and support.

With Saturn (7) as the Ruler in its own House, he/she has logical thinking and reasoning, and can accumulate things, using the skills to help in achievements.

With Rahu (8) as the Ruler in its own House, he/she is street smart, good at cultivating social friends, seeking fame, and using that skill to help obtain assistance and support from others.

Pseudo Rulers *(Anukaset)*

In a person's birth chart, sometimes two or more planets swap positions in the Ruler's signs of each other. They are called

Pseudo Rulers, meaning that they will exhibit the good quality typical of each individual planet but only after a long wait, or later in the life of the person. He/she has to undergo many trials and errors before the eventual success.

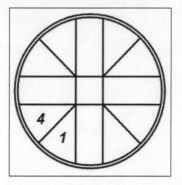

The Sun (1), Ruler of Leo, swaps positions with Mercury (4), Ruler of Virgo (two-way swap)

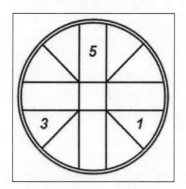

The Sun (1), Ruler of Leo, swaps positions with Jupiter (5), Ruler of Sagittarius, and with Mars (3), Ruler of Aries (three-way swap)

Exalted positions and Fall positions (Uj and Nij)

The planet that is Exalted in a particular sign appears brightest when it transits into that sign: for example, the Sun (1) in Aries during the spring season. In this position, its astrological quality is highest. On the other hand, when it transits through the sign directly opposite, for example the Sun (1) in Libra which occurs during the fall season, the Sun appears least bright. In this position, its astrological quality is lowest.

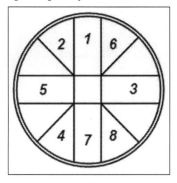

Planets in Exalted positions

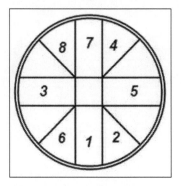

Planets in Fall positions

The Exalted planets in the zodiac signs just before attaining the Exalted positions are called Pre Exalted positions. The planets in the signs just after are called Post Exalted positions. They are also strong but a little less than when they are in the Exalted positions. But when they are in the sign where they also have other positions, those other positions prevail over Pre or Post Exalted positions. For example, the Moon (2) in Aries is in both

Assistance position and Pre Exalted position. Therefore, read it only as Assistance position. However, there are no Pre or Post positions for Ruler positions, Perseverance positions or Assistance positions.

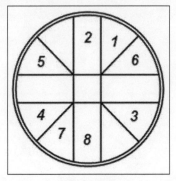

Planets in Pre Exalted positions

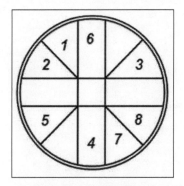

Planets in Post Exalted positions

Perseverance positions and Assistance positions *(Mahajak and Rajachoke)*

Planets in certain signs exhibit the quality of Perseverance. Their good quality seems to work overtime. They give the person the good quality in an exciting, exhilarating way. The results tend to be exponential, with sudden and unexpected success; which may be in having physical attractiveness in case of the Moon (2), or career advancement resulting from high ability and hard work in the case of Mars (3), for example. The Assistance planets give the person the personality that wins support from others, especially from people in authority or people with resources.

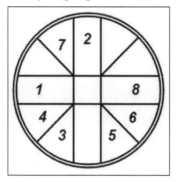

Planets in Perseverance positions

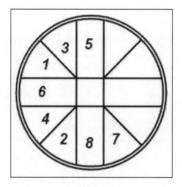

Planets in Assistance positions

Perseverance positions and Assistance positions – Queen Size *(Julajak and Devichoke)*

Planets that are directly opposite the Perseverance positions are called Perseverance positions – Queen Size. They are still beneficial, but of lesser quality than the former. The same with planets in Assistance positions – Queen Size. They seem to exert their good quality most when they are in the same House with Lagna, therefore should be used only as supplementary information.

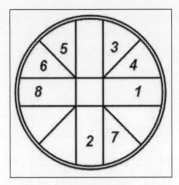

Planets in Perseverance positions
Queen Size

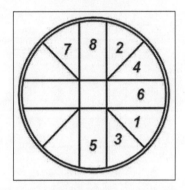

Planets in Assistance positions
Queen Size

7. The Aspect of the Planets

The Aspect of planets is when one planet reaches another and thus exerts influence, imposing its quality and characteristics, on the other. The second planet takes on some of the quality, both good and bad, from the first planet. There are many ways that the planets can aspect or reach each other. An example of the way the planets influence each other in Princess Diana's birth chart is in Part IV, Second Reading of the Birth Chart.

Conjunction

This is when one planet is in the same zodiac sign (same House) with the other. Planets in the same House react to each other, even though their positions may not be in exactly the same spot in degrees and minutes. As with the planet, the same goes with Lagna. Whichever planet resides in the first (Self) House with Lagna will have a lot of influence over Lagna, and the person's life. The influence from conjunction is a hundred per cent of force.

Opposite

This is when one planet is in the House directly opposite another, or opposite Lagna. Here the influence is as strong as conjunction at a hundred per cent.

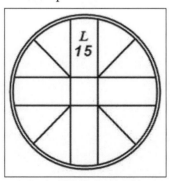

Planets in conjunction with Lagna in Aries

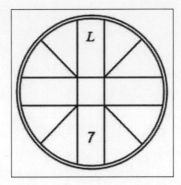

Planet that is opposite to Lagna in Aries

Trine

This is when one planet is five Houses from the other, counting the House in which it resides as the first House. For example, the planet in Aries is in trine with the planets in Leo and Sagittarius. The influence is less than conjunction and opposite. For the sake of explanation, it is roughly equated to seventy-five per cent.

Sextile

This is when one planet is either three Houses or eleven Houses from the other, counting the House in which it resides as the first House. For example, the planet in Aries is in sextile with the planets in Gemini and Aquarius. The influence can be considered to be about fifty to seventy-five per cent.

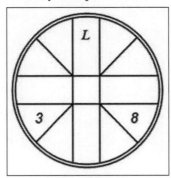

Planets that are in trine with Lagna

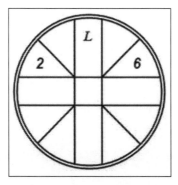

Planets that are in sextile with Lagna

Right angles

This is when there are one or more planets in the fourth (Home) House from Lagna, and the seventh (Spouse) House, and the tenth (Career) House. The influence of all planets at right angles to each other and to Lagna is quite strong because they are in the important Houses of life matter. It also applies in relation to any planet when there are planets four Houses, and seven Houses and ten Houses from that planet. For example, if there are planets in Aquarius, Taurus, Leo and Scorpio, they can all reach each other.

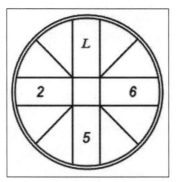

**Planets at right angles
to Lagna in Aries**

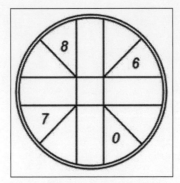

Venus (6) is adversely affected
By three Maleficent planets

Clamp

There are two types of Clamp.

The first is when a planet has two other planets almost opposite: one in the sixth House from itself and another in the eighth House from itself. This Clamp is like an arrow pointing back at that planet. These two planets together can exert their influences on that planet strongly. The effect, either good or bad, is even more intense if there is another planet of the same kind (Beneficent/Maleficent) in the same House with the first planet, forming a perfect arrow.

If the planets of clamp are Maleficent planets, then the influences on the target planet is bad, and vice versa for the Beneficent planets. This is especially so when the target planet is the planet in the birth chart and the other planets involved are the planets in transit.

The second type is when the target planet has two other planets on either side: one in the second House from itself and another in the twelfth House from itself. The same principles also apply when the target is Lagna instead of a planet.

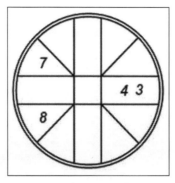

Mercury (4) is in arrow clamped by
Mars (3), Saturn (7) and Rahu (8)

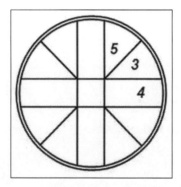

Mars (3) is clamped by Jupiter (5)
and Mercury (4) on either side

Special reach of Mars (3), Jupiter (5) and Saturn (7)

There are also exceptions with Mars (3), Jupiter (5) and Saturn (7).

Mars (3) can influence the planets that are four Houses and eight Houses away with equal (hundred per cent) influence. Jupiter (5) can influence the planets that are five Houses and nine Houses away with equal (hundred per cent) influence. Saturn (7) can influence the planets that are three Houses and ten Houses away with equal (hundred per cent) influence.

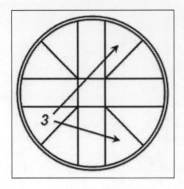
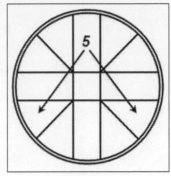

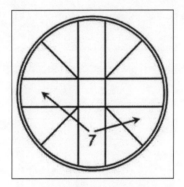

Special reach of planets in the signs with common rulers

When a planet is in the zodiac sign that has a common Ruler with another sign, it automatically reaches any planet that is in the other sign. For example, a planet is Aries can reach the planet in Scorpio. For the sake of explanation, the force can be roughly equated to twenty-five per cent.

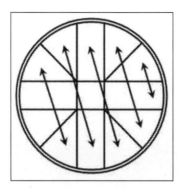

Cardinal signs, Fixed signs and Mutable signs

Cardinal signs, which are Aries, Cancer, Libra and Capricorn, are signs of rapid movement. Planets in these signs exert their good and bad quality more quickly than when they are in other types of sign.

Fixed signs, which are Taurus, Leo, Scorpio and Aquarius, are signs of slow movement. Planets in these signs indicate endurance and permanence.

Mutable signs, which are Gemini, Virgo, Sagittarius and Pisces, are signs of uncertainty, instability and changeability. Planets in these signs enable the person to embrace changes.

Part III:

First Reading of the Birth Chart

Your birth chart tells a story. The way that each planet exerts influence on each House in the chart, and on each other, dictates your characteristic and behavior. They in turn influence your future life.

8. Basic concepts

Ruler positions, Exalted positions, Perseverance positions or Assistance positions

The strength and influence of a planet is high if it is in Ruler position, Exalted position, Perseverance position or Assistance position, and low if it is in Insecure position and Fall position.

When the Ruler of a Benefic House is in another Benefic House, it brings its good quality to that House. If that planet is strong, the tendency for success is enhanced. If that planet is weak, the opposite will happen.

When the Ruler of a Malefic House (which are the sixth (Enemy) House, the eight (Death) House and the twelfth (Loss) House) is in a Benefic House; it brings its bad quality to that House. If that planet is strong, the damage is heavier. If that planet is weak, the damage is lighter.

However, when the Ruler of a Malefic House is in its own House, its good quality is still potent. The person may suffer some harm in matters related to that House but it tends to be mild. Or the issue related to that Malefic House may face some initial difficulties, but will turn out well eventually.

For example, if the Ruler of the sixth (Enemy) House is in its own House, it makes the person cautious against excesses and looks after him/herself well. If the Ruler of the eighth (Death) House is in its own House, it makes the person understand the nature and the circle of life, and guard him/her against morbidity. If the Ruler of the twelfth (Loss) House is in its own House, it makes the person cautious, and guards him/her against sudden calamity.

The only exception is when the Moon (2) or Jupiter (5) is in the eighth (Death) House which is the Special Position of Hardship, to be explained later. Even when these two planets are in Ruler position in its own House, the adverse affect will still occur.

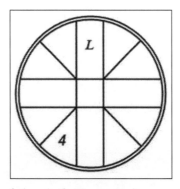

Ruler of the sixth House in its own House

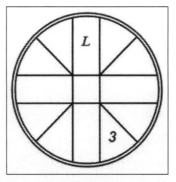

Ruler of the eighth House in its own House

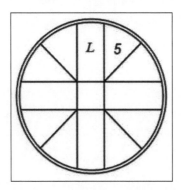

Ruler of the twelfth House in its own House

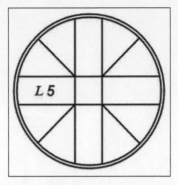

Ruler of the sixth House in Exalted position

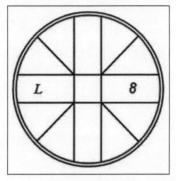

Ruler of the eighth House in Perseverance position

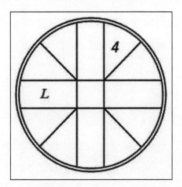

Ruler of the twelfth House in Fall position

Recovery of Insecure positions, Fall positions

The planet in Insecure position can be recovered if;

A. It is opposite another planet that is also in Insecure position (for example, Mars (3) in Libra with Venus (6) in Aries), or

B. It is in conjunction with a planet in Exalted position, or

C. It is opposite a planet in Exalted position, or

D. It is in a House whose Ruler is in Exalted position.

The recovery is only just to take the Insecure planets back to neutral, however, and not to raise their strength to the Ruler position.

The planet in Fall position can also be recovered if;

A. It is opposite another planet that is also in Fall position (for example, the Sun (1) in Libra with Saturn (7) in Aries), or

B. It is in conjunction with a planet in Ruler position, or

C. It is opposite a planet in Ruler position, or

D. It is in a House whose Ruler is in Ruler position, or

E. In the House where it is a Co-Ruler, there is a Co-Ruler in Ruler position in its own House (for example, Rahu (8) in Fall position in Taurus with Saturn (7) in Aquarius).

The recovery is not just to take the Fall planets back to neutral, however, but to raise their strength to the Ruler positions.

Two minuses equal a plus

The rule of two minuses equaling a plus holds true in many respect in Thai Astrology. When the Ruler of one Malefic House (the sixth (Enemy) House, the eighth (Death) House and the twelfth (Loss) House) is in another Malefic House, the net effect is neutral. The bad influence of that planet is neutralized. Also when the Ruler of a Malefic House is weak because it is in

Insecure position or Fall position, the bad quality of that planet is neutralized.

When the Ruler of a Benefic House is in a Malefic House, the matter related to that planet is negative. But if it is in Insecure position or Fall position, the negative becomes neutral.

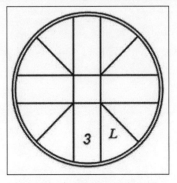

**Ruler of the sixth House
in the twelfth House**

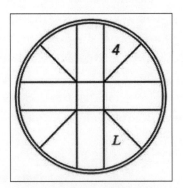

**Ruler of the eighth House
in Fall position**

The affect of two planets in Exalted positions that are opposite each other can sometimes cancel out the good quality of each other. The same can happen when there are many planets in Exalted positions in the birth chart. Planets in Exalted positions are especially strong and will try to dominate other planets. They may end up harming each other. They could lead to a temporary success followed by an eventual failure. This is not the same with planets in Ruler positions. There can never be too many planets in Ruler position since they all lead to security and permanency.

9. The Effect of the Houses on Each Other

To read about an issue; first, you identify which House to read. Second, see what planet is the Ruler of that House. Third, see where that planet is situated. The issue asked about the first House is answered by the House occupied by that planet.

For example, if you want to read about Self (which is subject of the first House), you first identify which planet is the Ruler of the zodiac sign that is the first House. Suppose Lagna is in Aries. The Ruler of Aries is Mars (3). Next, you locate Mars (3) in the birth chart. Whichever House in which Mars (3) occupies will tell you the story about Self. It indicates the matters that the person (self) is most preoccupied with. Suppose Mars (3) is with Lagna in Aries, then the Ruler of the first (Self) House is in its own House *(Self into Self)*. If Mars (3) is in Taurus instead, then the Ruler of the first (Self) House is in the second (Income) House *(Self into Income)*.

You also have to see the strength of the planet involved. If it is in Ruler position, Exalted position, Enhancement position or Assistance position, it is strong. Even if it is not, its strength may still be enhanced if it is in the House where the Ruler of that House is its Friendly Pair, Element Pair or Enhancement Pair. The opposite applies if it is in Insecure position, Fall position or in a House where the Ruler of that House is its Enemy Pair.

Ruler of the first (Self) House
The person will be preoccupied with the matter related to the House in which the Ruler of the first (Self) House occupies. The following lists the effect when the Ruler of the first (Self) House occupies each of the twelve Houses:

In the first (Self) House: The Ruler is in its own House *(Self into Self)*. The person will be preoccupied with self development. He/she is receptive to suggestions and criticism and uses them to refine him/herself. He/she is self confident, hard working and diligent, although he/she may face an initial period of hard work and struggle.

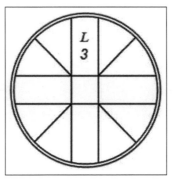

Ruler of the first House
is in its own House

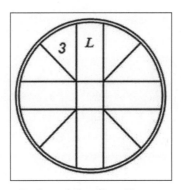

Ruler of the first House
is in the second House

In the second (Income) House *(Self into Income)*: The person is preoccupied with earning money. He/she is prepared to make sacrifices, be flexible to adapt and change, in order to make his/her income secured. To him/her, money is a very important consideration.

In the third (Friend) House *(Self into Friend)*: The person is preoccupied with close friends, work colleagues and siblings.

This is not the type of person that prefers to relax at home alone.

In the fourth (Home) House *(Self into Home)*: The person values relationship with relatives. His/her upbringing is warm and happy. His/her priorities are with his/her own home.

In the fifth (Children) House *(Self into Children)*: The person is preoccupied with his/her children or younger people. He/she loves the lime light, romantic and social affairs, affluence, new ideas and innovation, and is frequently lucky from speculation.

In the sixth (Enemy) House *(Self into Enemy)*: The person likes challenging situations and problems. He/she is not afraid of enemies or difficulties. He/she may be a competitive or combative sportsperson.

In the seventh (Spouse) House *(Self into Spouse)*: The Ruler is in Insecure position. The person seeks out spouse, is preoccupied with his/her spouse or business partner. He/she is considerate in marriage and subordinates his/her priorities to those of his/her spouse.

In the eighth (Death) House *(Self into Death)*: The person is weak or unhealthy, or is preoccupied with separation, long range traveling, or settlement abroad. He/she tends to make more success abroad than at home. He/she can build wealth and status after marriage, since if you start from the seventh (Spouse) House; this is the second House of income of his/her spouse.

In the ninth (Exalted) House *(Self into Exaltation)*: The person is preoccupied with progress and the attainment of honor. He/she is successful in dealing with elders, foreign parties, and in academics. He/she wants to be a successful head of his/her own family.

In the tenth (Career) House *(Self into Career)*: The person concentrates entirely on work, or making big investments, trying to be the owner of his/her own business. He/she is committed, highly responsible and reliable in performing tasks. His/her job more or less dictates his/her life.

In the eleventh (Luck) House *(Self into Luck)*: The person is good at finding support and success in endeavors. He/she learns quickly how to win help. He/she always calculates financial return. This is a good indication of the ability to accumulate wealth.

In the twelfth (Loss) House *(Self into Loss)*: The person prefers a quiet life. He/she is not expressive, feeling uncomfortable in social functions. He/she works better as an advisor behind the scene, prone to suffering losses, and tending to be bound in secrets.

Ruler of the second (Income) House

In the first (Self) House: The effect is similar to having the Ruler of the first (Self) House in the second (Income) House. The person is preoccupied with earning money. The possibility of success is higher in this situation than the former.

In the second (Income) House: The Ruler is in its own House. The person concentrates on having a regular and secure source of income. He/she is careful in taking risks, good at personal financial management, leading to a successful family life.

In the third (Friend) House: The person looks to his/her close friends or siblings for his/her income source so he/she has to be careful in the relationship with them.

In the fourth (Home) House: The person looks to his/her parents or relatives for his/her income source. He/she is good at work related to real estate or in accumulating wealth in the form of real estate.

In the fifth (Children) House: The person works with children or younger people, or his/her income source is related to young people. He/she invests money on his/her children's education and upbringing. He/she tends to be lucky in gambling or speculation.

In the sixth (Enemy) House: The person may have difficulty in maintaining his/her source of income. Or he/she may be too free with spending, and easily drawn into debts. Or his/her source of income may be related to his/her enemies, such as from professional boxing.

In the seventh (Spouse) House: The person wants to work with his/her spouse or business partner for a income source. He/she may join in business projects with the relatives of his/her spouse.

In the eighth (Death) House: The Ruler is in Insecure position. The person is careless in spending. Or he/she may neglect developing skills to earn a living. Or he/she may come into wealth through matters related to death, such as inheritance.

In the ninth (Exalted) House: The person relies on his/her position or foreign dealings, or support from elders or parents for his/her work or income source.

In the tenth (Career) House: The person's income source is solely from work.

In the eleventh (Luck) House: The person is good at finding support and assistance from others. He is good at spotting opportunities. This is another good indication of a man of wealth.

In the twelfth (Loss) House: The person may lose his/her income due to sudden, fraudulent, unforeseen or secretive causes. He/she has to be especially careful in money management. Or he/she may be the type who likes to hide his/her wealth.

Ruler of the third (Friend) House

In the first (Self) House: The effect is similar to having the Ruler of the first (Self) House in the third (Friend) House: The person allows his/her close friends to become involved in his/her affairs. He/she is likely to take frequent short trips.

In the second (Income) House: The person has to give financial support to his/her close friends or siblings. They generally look to him/her for help.

In the third (Friend) House: The Ruler is in its own House. The person enjoys the company of friends and siblings. His/her relationship with them is long lasting. His/her close friends tend to be of high society.

In the fourth (Home) House: The person treats his/her friends like close relatives. He/she also maintains a close relationship with relatives.

In the fifth (Children) House: The person enjoys the company and friendship of younger people, or work subordinates. His/her friends and siblings may become closely involved with his/her children.

In the sixth (Enemy) House: The person has difficulty in the relationship with close friends and siblings. Eventually they turn into enemies. He/she may also be accident prone in short travel in vehicles.

In the seventh (Spouse) House: The person tends to marry a close friend, or may find his/her spouse through contact with friends, or his/her relationship with his/her spouse is like a friend.

In the eighth (Death) House: The person has difficulty seeking help from his/her friends and siblings, or they tend to bring difficulty, or he/she may outlive them. He/she may also be accident prone in short travel in vehicles.

In the ninth (Exalted) House: The Ruler is in Insecure position. The person tends to select close friends people that are in honorable positions, or foreigners, but the friendship may be insecure.

In the tenth (Career) House: The person likes to have close friends or siblings involved in his/her career.

In the eleventh (Luck) House: The person finds support from close friends or siblings for work. They tend to bring luck.

In the twelfth (Loss) House: The person tends to be separated from close friends or siblings, or they may betray him/her or bring difficulties.

Ruler of the fourth (Home) House

In the first (Self) House: The effect is similar to having the Ruler of the first (Self) House in the fourth (Home) House. The person welcomes parents and relatives into daily affairs.

In the second (Income) House: The person has to give financial support to parents or relatives. He/she may over spend on acquiring vehicles and homes.

In the third (Friend) House: The effect is similar to having the Ruler of the third (Friend) House in the fourth (Home) House. The person enjoys visit with friends.

In the fourth (Home) House: The Ruler is in its own House. The person has a strong clan with secured background. He/she enjoys financial support from parents and is good at accumulating real estate.

In the fifth (Children) House: The person gets on well with his/her children and young people. Or his/her children may be financially supported by his/her parents and relatives. Or they may grow up under their care.

In the sixth (Enemy) House: The person has difficulty with parents and relatives. He/she may change jobs often or run the risk of litigations. For a man, he could be separated from his mother at an early age, and for the woman, the father.

In the seventh (Spouse) House: The person finds a spouse through introduction by the family, or the spouse may be his/her distant relative, or he/she may treat a spouse like a relative. Real estate tends to be held in the name of his/her spouse.

In the eighth (Death) House: The person outlives relatives, or may have few relatives, or may face difficulties caused by relatives. The person may also resettle abroad.

In the ninth (Exalted) House: The person's parents are of high society or have such friends. They provide a warm and strong upbringing.

In the tenth (Career) House: The person works in a family business, or projects linked to relatives, or the job with their support. The work, however, tends to be static, because the Ruler is in Insecure position.

In the eleventh (Luck) House: The person receives support from parents and relatives. They tend to bring him/her luck. He/she is good at accumulating wealth and assets. He/she will also do well in jobs related to real estate.

In the twelfth (Loss) House: The person tends to be separated from parents and relatives, or has difficulty holding on to wealth, or faces difficulties caused by relatives. He/she is forced to uproot his/her dwelling often.

Ruler of the fifth (Children) House

In the first (Self) House: The effect is similar to having the Ruler of the first (Self) House in the fifth (Children) House. The person allows his/her children or younger people to be closely involved with his/her life.

In the second (Income) House: The person has to spend money to support his/her children or younger people. He/she may the type to spoil children with too much allowance.

In the third (Friend) House: The effect is similar to having the Ruler of the third (Friend) House in the fifth (Children) House. The person treats children as close friends.

In the fourth (Home) House: The effect is similar to having the Ruler of the fourth (Home) House in the fifth (Children) House. His/her children are close to relatives.

In the fifth (Children) House: The Ruler is in its own House. The relationship between the person and his/her children is secure and stable. Priority is given to developing children, hence their better chances of success.

In the sixth (Enemy) House: The person has difficulty with his/her children, or may have few children, or they may bring difficulties.

In the seventh (Spouse) House: The person marries a much younger spouse, or marries at a very young age, or marries his/her work assistant.

In the eighth (Death) House: The person dislikes children or has difficulty dealing with them, or is without children or tends to be separated from his/her children.

In the ninth (Exalted) House: The person is devoted to his/her children, and they are also successful. His/her children excel in studying, or work in high positions or work abroad.

In the tenth (Career) House: The person's children are involved in his/her work, or he/she may have to support children in their work.

In the eleventh (Luck) House: The person is lucky in speculation. He/she is devoted to his/her children, happy with them around. The family finance may become stronger after having children. His/her work subordinates give support. However, the Ruler is in Insecure position, making the good quality insecure.

In the twelfth (Loss) House: The person is separated from his/her children, or they may bring difficulties, or live far away from each other.

Ruler of the sixth (Enemy) House

In the first (Self) House: The person is ineffective at defending him/herself, or is easily taken advantage of. His/her character may risk being untrustworthy.

In the second (Income) House: The person often finds opportunities frustrated by enemies, or over spends money or builds up too much debt.

In the third (Friend) House: The effect is similar to having the Ruler of the third (Friend) House in the sixth (enemy) House. The person has difficulties caused by close friends or siblings, or from short journeys.

In the fourth (Home) House: The effect is similar to having the Ruler of the fourth (Home) House in the sixth (enemy) House. The person has difficulties caused by elders or relatives.

In the fifth (Children) House: The effect is similar to having the Ruler of the fifth (Children) House in the sixth (enemy) House. The person has difficulties caused by children.

In the sixth (Enemy) House: The Ruler is in its own House. The person tends to avoid having enemies, but if there is one it tends to last a long time. He/she is generally healthy, but should he/she fall ill, the illness also tends to last a long time.

In the seventh (Spouse) House: The effect is similar to having the Ruler of the seventh (Spouse) House in the sixth (enemy) House. The person has difficulties caused by his/her spouse or business partners. Or he/she may remain forever single, or face the risk of divorce.

In the eighth (Death) House: The person is healthy throughout life, or should he/she falls ill, will recover quickly. He/she may be good at avoiding enemies or in dealing with enemies.

In the ninth (Exalted) House: The person has difficulties from parents, elders or from fighting over inheritance. His/her promotion and progress in work may be slow or frustrated. He/she does not get much support from people in high authority.

In the tenth (Career) House: The person tends to have difficulty in work or conflict within business. He/she seems to constantly attract enemies and opposition.

In the eleventh (Luck) House: The person has difficulties in his/her source of income or has to share it with others. He/she tends to be unsuccessful in gambling. Or lucky breaks come only after a struggle.

In the twelfth (Loss) House: The person risks having difficulties caused by people close to him/her. However, he/she is good at handling enemies. He/she also tends to be healthy throughout life.

Ruler of the seventh (Spouse) House

In the first (Self) House: Because the Ruler of the seventh (Spouse) House is in Insecure position, his/her spouse can be of

75

a lower social position than him/herself, or the returned attraction may not be permanent, or the courtship period is too long and marriage may not materialize.

In the second (Income) House: His/her spouse exhausts his/her wealth. The person faces difficulties caused by the spouse and he/she can also have more than one spouse.

In the third (Friend) House: The effect is similar to having the Ruler of the third (Friend) House in the seventh (Spouse) House. The person chooses his/her close friend for a spouse. In some cases, the relationship remains at friendship level and the person never marries.

In the fourth (Home) House: The effect is similar to having the Ruler of the fourth (Home) House in the seventh (Spouse) House. The person accepts a spouse introduced to him/her by elders or relatives, or his/her spouse may get on very well with relatives.

In the fifth (Children) House: The effect is similar to having the Ruler of the fifth (Children) House in the seventh (Spouse) House. The person treats his/her spouse like his/her children. He/she may try to control his/her spouse too much. Or his/her spouse may be much younger.

In the sixth (Enemy) House: The effect is similar to having the Ruler of the sixth (Enemy) House in the seventh (Spouse) House. The person has difficulties with the spouse.

In the seventh (Spouse) House: The Ruler is in its own House. The person is successful in marriage, living together until old age. He/she is careful in selecting his/her spouse with regard to financial, social and educational background.

In the eighth (Death) House: The person's marital passion wears off after some time. He/she may live away from his/her spouse or could possibly be divorced or widowed. His/her marriage may be late in life, or may not occur at all. He/she finds difficulties in business with partners.

In the ninth (Exalted) House: The person selects a spouse with a good background, and respects him/her, or may choose a spouse from high society, or from abroad.

In the tenth (Career) House: The person concentrates on work at the expense of marriage, or his/her career may heavily involve the opposite sex. His/her spouse may help with his/her work.

In the eleventh (Luck) House: The person selects a spouse based on wealth or income. His/her spouse brings luck and the marriage is smooth. He/she may also have more than one spouse.

In the twelfth (Loss) House: The person faces difficulties caused by his/her spouse, or his/her lifestyle may become restricted and constrained after marriage, or he/she is separated from the spouse.

Ruler of the eighth (Death) House

In the first (Self) House: The effect is similar to having the Ruler of the first (Self) House in the eighth (Death) House. The person is physically weak and infirm and may suffer from poor memory that adversely affects work. Or his/her work may involve dealing with foreigners.

In the second (Income) House: The Ruler is in Insecure position and therefore lessens the bad effect related to death. He/she takes time to build wealth. However, the person tends to receive inheritance or sudden unexpected income.

In the third (Friend) House: The effect is similar to having the Ruler of the third (Friend) House in the eighth (Death) House. The person is parted from close friends or siblings. Or he/she has to make regular short journeys.

In the fourth (Home) House: The effect is similar to having the Ruler of the fourth (Home) House in the eighth (Death) House. The person is separated from relatives.

In the fifth (Children) House: The effect is similar to having the Ruler of the fifth (Children) House in the eighth (Death) House. The person has difficulty having children, or his/her children risk having major illnesses.

In the sixth (Enemy) House: The effect is similar to having the

Ruler of the sixth (Enemy) House in the eighth (Death) House. The person is good at managing enemies.

In the seventh (Spouse) House: The effect is similar to having the Ruler of the seventh (Spouse) House in the eighth (Death) House. The person faces difficulties caused by his/her spouse, or the spouse may risk having major illness.

In the eighth (Death) House: The Ruler is in its own House. The person is of strong build, careful about diet and health. He/she may also have a high chance of receiving inheritance from his/her spouse.

If the Ruler is in its own House in the eighth (Death) House, the adverse affect is neutralized, except when it is the Moon (2) or Jupiter (5). The Moon (2) deprives the person of a good look and good manner. Jupiter (5) can make the person immoral and dishonest.

In the ninth (Exalted) House: The person has difficulty seeking support from elders, parents, and may have separated from parents at an early age. His/her own family can also suffer from illness and death.

In the tenth (Career) House: The person often faces difficult challenges in work, or has to change jobs too often. However, this is a good position for people in the medical services, or work related to death.

In the eleventh (Luck) House: The person has difficulties seeking support from others. However, he/she may find luck related to foreign activities or inheritance.

In the twelfth (Loss) House: The person is healthy throughout life. He/she is quick at recovering loss, correcting a bad situation, or from an illness.

Ruler of the ninth (Exalted) House
In the first (Self) House: The effect is similar to having the Ruler of the first (Self) House in the ninth (Exaltation) House.
The person is successful in dealing with foreign parties, and good

at academics. His/her chance of success is stronger here than in the former.

In the second (Income) House: The effect is similar to having the Ruler of the second (Income) House in the ninth (Exaltation) House. The person receives income support from elders or parents, or wealth may be from his/her position.

In the third (Friend) House: The effect is similar to having the Ruler of the third (Friend) House in the ninth (Exaltation) House. The person selects close friends in honored positions or foreigners. However, the Ruler is in Insecure position, making the elders insincere and inconsistent in their support.

In the fourth (Home) House: The effect is similar to having the Ruler of the fourth (Home) House in the ninth (Exaltation) House. The person comes from a family clan with high social standing.

In the fifth (Children) House: The effect is similar to having the Ruler of the fifth (Children) House in the ninth (Exaltation) House. The person's children are successful.

In the sixth (Enemy) House: The effect is similar to having the Ruler of the sixth (Enemy) House in the ninth (Exaltation) House. The person has difficulty with elders. He/she may also face many opponents in work.

In the seventh (Spouse) House: The effect is similar to having the Ruler of the seventh (Spouse) House in the ninth (Exaltation) House. The person marries up.

In the eighth (Death) House: The effect is similar to having the Ruler of the eighth (Death) House in the ninth (Exaltation) House. The person finds difficulty seeking support from elders.

In the ninth (Exalted) House: The Ruler is in its own House. The person concentrates on honor and achievement. He/she easily wins support of elders and people in high authority. He/she enjoys a close relationship with parent (father in the case of man, and mother in case of woman), and excels in foreign dealings.

In the tenth (Career) House: The person finds honor from work. He/she is good at work related to administration and leadership. He/she achieves high career success.

In the eleventh (Luck) House: The person is good at finding support from elders, parents, friends and colleagues. People in higher positions give support and often bring luck.

In the twelfth (Loss) House: The person has the risk of suddenly losing position or honor. There is a risk of public scandal or criticism.

Ruler of the tenth (Career) House

In the first (Self) House: The effect is similar to having the Ruler of the first (Self) House in the tenth (Career) House. The person gives high priority to work.

In the second (Income) House: The person may deplete wealth or income to try to support work or projects. He/she tends to over invest.

In the third (Friend) House: The effect is similar to having the Ruler of the third (Friend) House in the tenth (Career) House. The person has close friends or siblings involved in his/her career.

In the fourth (Home) House: The effect is similar to having the Ruler of the fourth (Home) House in the tenth (Career) House. The person works with relatives or in the job with their support. The Ruler is in Insecure position, which restricts the expansion of work.

In the fifth (Children) House: The effect is similar to having the Ruler of the fifth (Children) House in the tenth (Career) House. The person lets his/her children become involved in his/her work.

In the sixth (Enemy) House: The effect is similar to having the Ruler of the sixth (Enemy) House in the tenth (Career) House. The person finds enemies in work or faces conflicts within business.

In the seventh (Spouse) House: The effect is similar to having the Ruler of the seventh (Spouse) House in the tenth (Career) House. The person involves his/her spouse in work.

In the eighth (Death) House: The effect is similar to having the Ruler of the eighth (Death) House in the tenth (Career) House. The person faces difficulties in work.

In the ninth (Exalted) House: The effect is similar to having the Ruler of the ninth (Exalted) House in the tenth (Career) House. The person finds honor from work.

In the tenth (Career) House: The Ruler is in its own House. The person's career is secured. He/she is flexible and adaptable, therefore can surpass difficulties and setbacks and hold on to his/her career for a long time.

In the eleventh (Luck) House: The person achieves great success in work. His/her work brings security and wealth.

In the twelfth (Loss) House: The person often faces difficulties related to work. He/she may have to change jobs often.

Ruler of the eleventh (Luck) House

In the first (Self) House: The effect is similar to having the Ruler of the first (Self) House in the eleventh (Luck) House. The person finds ready support from others and is successful in life. This is another strong indication of wealth.

In the second (Income) House: The effect is similar to having the Ruler of the second (Income) House in the eleventh (Luck) House. The person is particularly good at spotting financial opportunities. This is another strong indication of wealth.

In the third (Friend) House: The effect is similar to having the Ruler of the third (Friend) House in the eleventh (Luck) House. The person finds support from close friends or siblings.

In the fourth (Home) House: The effect is similar to having the Ruler of the fourth (Home) House in the eleventh (Luck) House. The person receives support from parents and relatives. He/she is good at work related to real estate.

In the fifth (Children) House: The effect is similar to having the Ruler of the fifth (Children) House in the eleventh (Luck) House. The person tends to be lucky in speculation, or activities related to children or youth. However, the Ruler is in Insecure position, making the results insecure or the benefits less than anticipated.

In the sixth (Enemy) House: The person finds success through struggles or competitive sports, or from antiquities. However, he/she has to put in a lot of efforts and may have to wait a long time for success.

In the seventh (Spouse) House: The effect is similar to having the Ruler of the seventh (Spouse) House in the eleventh (Luck) House. The person's marriage tends to be smooth. He/she may marry up, or has many partners.

In the eighth (Death) House: The effect is similar to having the Ruler of the eighth (Death) House in the eleventh (Luck) House. The person finds luck in unforeseen things, or finds benefits related to certain losses.

In the ninth (Exalted) House: The effect is similar to having the Ruler of the ninth (Exalted) House in the eleventh (Luck) House. The person finds support from elders or parents.

In the tenth (Career) House: The effect is similar to having the Ruler of the tenth (Career) House in the eleventh (Luck) House. The person has a very successful career.

In the eleventh (Luck) House: The Ruler is in its own House. The person is successful and always lucky. He/she is good at securing support and backing from others.

In the twelfth (Loss) House: The person finds success through secret activities, or is better working behind the scene.

Ruler of the twelfth (Loss) House

In the first (Self) House: The effect is similar to having the Ruler of the first (Self) House in the twelfth (Loss) House. But in addition, the person may face the risk of detention, or extreme morbidity.

In the second (Income) House: The effect is similar to having the Ruler of the second (Income) House in the twelfth (Loss) House. The person faces the risk of bankruptcy, losing his/her income source or wealth due to fraudulent, sudden causes.

In the third (Friend) House: The effect is similar to having the Ruler of the third (Friend) House in the twelfth (Loss) House. The person is separated from close friends or siblings.

In the fourth (Home) House: The effect is similar to having the Ruler of the fourth (Home) House in the twelfth (Loss) House. The person is separated from parents and relatives, or has difficulty in holding on to real estate.

In the fifth (Children) House: The effect is similar to having the Ruler of the fifth (Children) House in the twelfth (Loss) House. The person is separated from his/her children. In a woman's chart, it can mean having an abortion or termination of pregnancy, or difficulty in conception or in childbirth.

In the sixth (Enemy) House: The person can evade difficulties or calamity. He/she is good at deflecting potential losses towards enemies instead of him/herself.

In the seventh (Spouse) House: The effect is similar to having the Ruler of the seventh (Spouse) House in the twelfth (Loss) House. The person risks facing difficulties from his/her spouse or partners, or be separated from his/her spouse. He/she may be overly active in romantic affairs.

In the eighth (Death) House: The effect is similar to having the Ruler of the eighth (Death) House in the twelfth (Loss) House. The person is healthy most of his/her life.

In the ninth (Exalted) House: The effect is similar to having the Ruler of the ninth (Exalted) House in the twelfth (Loss) House. The person has difficulties with elders or may have the risk of sudden loss of honor.

In the tenth (Career) House: The effect is similar to having the Ruler of the tenth (Career) House in the twelfth (Loss) House.

The person tends to have difficulties in work.

In the eleventh (Luck) House: The effect is similar to having the Ruler of the eleventh (Luck) House in the twelfth (Loss) House. The person struggles in finding support from others. Or luck may come from improper sources.

In the twelfth (Loss) House: The Ruler is in its own House. The person tends to be careful in avoiding losses and obstacles.

Ruler of the Houses in Insecure positions or Fall positions

Where the Ruler of a House is in Insecure position, the matter related to that House will be uncertain, impermanent, fluctuating. The result is smaller quantity, with the risk of postponement or delay caused by unresolved problems.

The effect of an Insecure planet on each House can be described as follow:

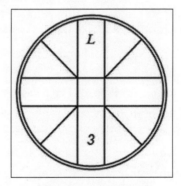

**Ruler of the first House
in Insecure position**

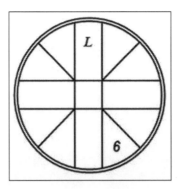

**Ruler of the second House
in Insecure position**

Ruler of the first (Self) House in Insecure position: The person can be too suspicious of his/her marriage partner. He/she may look weak or is constantly worried about his/her own health. Or may not be him/herself, being more prepared to subordinate priorities to others; for example, to his/her spouse or children.

Ruler of the second (Income) House: The person may have difficulty in maintaining an income, or he/she may over spend or commit to too many activities. Or he/she may risk depleting wealth.

Ruler of the third (Friend) House: The person tends to have few sibling, few close friends and cannot rely on them for help or assistance. His/her social circle is narrow and ineffective. He/she may also be inconsistent or insincere, straining the friendship.

Ruler of the fourth (Home) House: The person has difficulty in accumulating wealth. He/she cannot rely on relatives or parents. He/she is ineffective in attracting help. Or parents may be financially insecure, and he/she may have to move home often.

Ruler of the fifth (Children) House: The person may have very few children, or have difficulty in nurturing them. Or his/her children's achievement can be limited or uncertain.

Ruler of the sixth (Enemy) House: The person tends to be able to avoid making enemies. He/she is strong built. When he/she falls ill, recovery would occur in no time.

Ruler of the seventh (Spouse) House: The person allows his/her spouse to be involved in affairs closely. He/she may end up with someone in a lower social circle, or the love wears off after some time. Or marital life may suffer, and the risk of divorce is high. Or his/her partner may be insincere.

Ruler of the eighth (Death) House: The person tends to be healthy. Should he/she fall ill, he/she would recover in no time. He/she can come into inheritance later in life.

Ruler of the ninth (Exalted) House: The person cannot achieve honor or distinction. He/she has to help him/herself, unable to rely on much support from superiors or parents.

Ruler of the tenth (Career) House: The person changes job too readily. His/her line of work can be temporary, from one project to another. Or advancement can be slow.

Ruler of the eleventh (Luck) House: The person has difficulty finding success. He/she may wait only for the big breaks, while ignoring the small gains. Or he/she may be lucky in speculation, but it can come and go.

Ruler of the twelfth (Loss) House: The person is good at avoiding losses.

Where the Ruler of a House is in Fall position, the matter related to that House is poor, weak, partially damaged, soiled, antiquated, with deteriorating results, or can be part of immoral acts. The adverse affect can be sudden and heavy.

The effect of a Fall planet on each House can be described as follow:

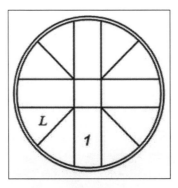

**Ruler of the first House
in Fall position**

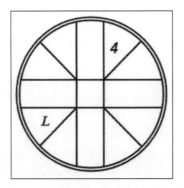

**Ruler of the second House
in Fall position**

Ruler of the first (Self) House in Fall position: The person can be susceptible to immoral suggestions. His/her will power and status will be low.

Ruler of the second (Income) House: The person risks seeking income from immoral activities, or risks depleting wealth. Or earnings are small.

Ruler of the third (Friend) House: The person risks being associated with siblings or close friends in immoral activities.

Ruler of the fourth (Home) House: The person may come from a weak background, insecure family, or parents of lower class or of poor health.

Ruler of the fifth (Children) House: The person's children or subordinates risks associating with people of shady background, immoral activities. Or they may also be of poor health.

Ruler of the sixth (Enemy) House: The person tends to be able to avoid making enemies. He/she is of strong built. When he/she falls ill, recovery would occur quickly. He/she is good at resolving his/her own problems.

Ruler of the seventh (Spouse) House: The person's spouse can be from a lower social class, or be involved in immoral acts, or be weak in health. Or he/she may suffer from fraudulent partners.

Ruler of the eighth (Death) House: The person tends to be healthy. Should he/she fall ill, recovery would occur quickly. He/she can come into inheritance, but it can be in the form of antiquities, or things in imperfect or poor conditions.

Ruler of the ninth (Exalted) House: The person has difficulty in seeking promotion and progress in work. There is also a risk of public scandals.

Ruler of the tenth (Career) House: The person risks failing in his/her job. Or his/her position may be unimportant or advancement can be slow.

Ruler of the eleventh (Luck) House: The person cannot achieve success, or may look to immoral sources for wealth, which tends to be small.

Ruler of the twelfth (Loss) House: The person tends to be careful in avoiding losses or making enemies. He/she is good at keeping secrets.

However, please note that the effects of Insecure or Fall planet described above are only preliminary and can still be recovered partly or wholly by other Beneficent planets.

Ruler of the Houses in Exalted positions, Perseverance positions or Assistance Positions

The Ruler of a Benefic House in Exalted positions, or Perseverance positions or Assistance Positions, will make the matter related to that House successful, just like the Ruler is in its own House. With the Exalted positions, the quality is at maximum. With the Perseverance positions, the good quality may start at a low level and increase exponentially. With the Assistance positions, the good quality comes through the help of others.

The Ruler of any of the Malefic House (the sixth, the eighth or the twelfth House) in Exalted positions and Perseverance positions worsens the bad quality related to that House. The Ruler of these Houses in Assistance positions does not worsen its bad quality, but its good quality is also absent. Similarly, if any of the Malefic Houses is occupied by a planet in Exalted position, it greatly increases the risks associated with that House. However, if it is occupied by a Perseverance planet or an Assistance planet, the risk is less.

An Exalted planet in the sixth (Enemy) House amplifies the risk from enemies. There can be numerous enemies or their power overwhelming. An exalted planet in the eighth (Death) House amplifies the risk of failure in work. An exalted planet in the twelfth (Loss) House amplifies the risk of unforeseen losses or sudden damage to assets.

10. Special Set Positions of the Planets

In Thai Astrology, certain combinations of planets, in relation to Lagna or Tanu Kaset, give unique predictable results.

The Special Positions for Success *(Ong Kaint)*
These combinations result in career success and financial comfort. They are classified according to the zodiac sign that Lagna occupies. The more planets in such position, the more they exert their good quality on each other.

Quadruped, which are the three signs of four-legged animals: Aries (ram), Taurus (bull), Leo (lion).

> *Quadruped with Jupiter in Ten*   *Life will tend to succeed*
> *Also Sun, Mars or Moon*   *These four sing successful tune*

Where Lagna is in Aries and there is one or more of the following planets in the tenth (Career) House from Lagna, which is Capricorn. The planets involved are the Sun (1), the Moon (2), Mars (3) and Jupiter (5).

Where Lagna is in Taurus and there is one or more of the following planets in the tenth (Career) House from Lagna, which is Aquarius. The planets involved are the Sun (1), the Moon (2), Mars (3) and Jupiter (5).

Where Lagna is in Leo and there is one or more of the following planets in the tenth (Career) House from Lagna, which is Taurus. The planets involved are the Sun (1), the Moon (2), Mars (3) and Jupiter (5).

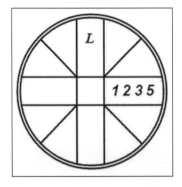
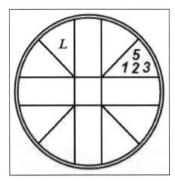

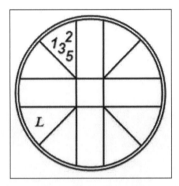

Human, which are the four signs of human form or utensils used by human: Gemini (twins), Virgo (virgin), Libra (balancing scale), Sagittarius (shooting arrow), Aquarius (water bottle).

> *Human signs with Jupiter in One*   *Give a brilliant run in life*
> *Also with Sun or Saturn*   *These three, failure will*
>   *spurn*

Where Lagna is in Gemini and there is one or more of the following planets also in Gemini, the first (self) House with Lagna. The planets involved are the Sun (1), Jupiter (5) and Saturn (7).

Where Lagna is in Virgo and there is one or more of the following planets also in Virgo, the first (Self) House with Lagna.

The planets involved are the Sun (1), Jupiter (5) and Saturn (7).

Where Lagna is in Libra and there is one or more of the following planets also in Libra, the first (self) House with Lagna. The planets involved are the Sun (1), Jupiter (5) and Saturn (7).

Where Lagna is in Sagittarius and there is one or more of the following planets also in Sagittarius, the first (Self) House with Lagna. The planets involved are the Sun (1), Jupiter (5) and Saturn (7).

Where Lagna is in Aquarius and there is one or more of the following planets also in Aquarius, the first (Self) House with Lagna. The planets involved are the Sun (1), Jupiter (5) and Saturn (7).

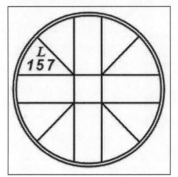 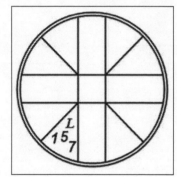

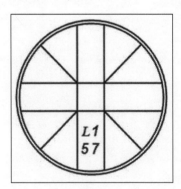

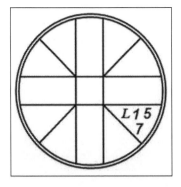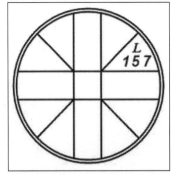

Aquatic, which are the three signs of marine animals: Cancer (crab), Capricorn (water snake), Pisces (fish).

Aquatic signs with Jupiter in Fourth	*Result in growth of life*
The four includes Mercury	*Venus and Moon for glory*

Where Lagna is in Cancer and there is one or more of the following planets in the fourth (Home) House from Lagna, which is Libra. The planets involved are the Moon (2), Mercury (4), Jupiter (5) and Venus (6).

Where Lagna is in Capricorn and there is one or more of the following planets in the fourth (Home) House from Lagna, which is Aries. The planets involved are the Moon (2), Mercury (4), Jupiter (5) and Venus (6).

Where Lagna is in Pisces and there is one or more of the following planets in the fourth (Home) House from Lagna, which is Gemini. The planets involved are the Moon (2), Mercury (4), Jupiter (5) and Venus (6).

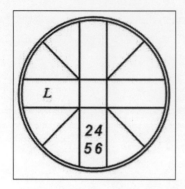
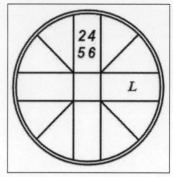
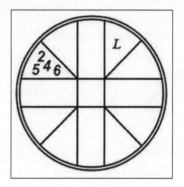

Scorpion, which is the only sign of insect: Scorpio (scorpion)

Scorpio with Rahu in Seventh　　　*As well as when there's*
　　　　　　　　　　　　　　　　Mars
These two planets in Seventh　　*Bring success to life by far*

Where Lagna is in Scorpio and there is one or more of the following planets in the seventh (Spouse) House from Lagna, which is Taurus. The planets involved are Mars (3) and Rahu (8).

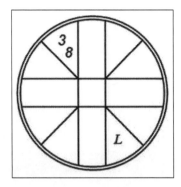

These combinations are especially beneficial if any of the planets involved are in a strong position (i.e. Ruler positions, Exalted positions, Perseverance positions or Assistance positions). On the other hand, the planets in weak positions (i.e. Insecure positions or Fall positions) will diminish the result. They apply both to the birth chart as well as to the planets in transit. For planets in transit, you have to examine their positions in relation to Lagna and in relation to the first (Self) House in transit, @, which will be explained later.

Why do these set positions give such good results?

The Houses involved (the first House (Self) in the Human group, the fourth House (Home) in the Aquatic group, the seventh House (Spouse) in the Scorpion group and the tenth House (Career) in the Quadruped group) are the most important Houses in our birth charts. They are the four most important aspects in our lives. Therefore, anyone with good habits and behavior in one or more of the four aspects tend to be successful in life.

The Special Omen planets *(Kaat)*

Later in the book, you will see that the first (Self) House also transits through the zodiac signs. This is denoted by @ in the transit chart. When @ is in a zodiac sign belonging to one of the four groups, certain planets are particularly adverse. They are called the Special Omen planets.

While @ is in Quadruped signs, it is Jupiter (5). In Human signs, it is Saturn (7). In Aquatic signs, it is Mars (3). In Scorpion sign, it is Rahu (8).

For example, suppose this year @ is in Aries, a Quadruped sign. For the period that @ is in Aries, Jupiter (5) is the Special Omen planet. When Jupiter (5) transits into the first (Self) House from Lagna, or into Aries in conjunction with @, the first (Self) House in transit, risks may occur to the person's health.

These planets are especially adverse when they are Kali in transit. The planet that represents Kali for a person changes every year on his/her birthday. This concept will be explained later in the chapter on Taksa. If in relation to @, the first (Self) House in transit, that planet is the Ruler of a Malefic House, the difficulties are greater.

The Special Positions of Plenty *(Udom Kaint)*

Similarly, the following combinations give the persons plenty of something. Plenty of what depends on the House that these planets occupy. They are also classified by group.

Quadruped: signs: Aries (ram), Taurus (bull), Leo (lion).

If in either the sixth (Enemy) House or the tenth (Career) House there is one or more of the following planets:

The Sun (1), the Moon (2), Mars (3) or Venus (6)

Human signs: Gemini (twins), Virgo (virgin), Libra (balancing scale), Sagittarius (shooting arrow), Aquarius (water bottle).

If in any of these Houses: the first (Self) House, the third (Friend) House, the fourth (Home) House, the seventh (Spouse) House or the eleventh (Luck) House; there is one or more of the following planets:

Mercury (4), Jupiter (5), Venus (6) or Saturn (7)

Aquatic signs: Cancer (crab), Capricorn (water snake), Pisces (fish).

If in any of these Houses: the fourth (Home) House, the fifth

(Children) House or the ninth (Exaltation) House; there is one or more of the following planets:

Mars (3), Jupiter (5), Saturn (7) or Rahu (8)

Scorpion signs: Scorpio (scorpion).

If in any of these Houses: the third (Friend) House, the seventh (Spouse) House, the ninth (Exaltation) House or the eleventh (Luck) House; there is either:

Mars (3) or Rahu (8)

The Special Combination of Sun Moon and Jupiter
(Suriya, Chandra, Guru)

This is where the Sun (1), the Moon (2) and Jupiter (5) are in any of the four cardinal signs (Aries, Cancer, Libra and Capricorn) in any combination. There must also be Lagna is one of the signs, or any one of these three planets is in conjunction with Lagna (or slightly less so if one of the three planets is instead in conjunction with the Ruler of the first (Self) House, or with Tanu-set).

Cardinal signs are the signs of quick movement. These three planets have good quality that become more effective in the cardinal signs, making the person successful. He/she is wealthy and can hold the highest political position. The best results are when the planets are also strong. In the example below, the Sun (1) is in Perseverance position, the Moon (2) although in Insecure position but is also in a special place in Capricorn, being the mother zodiac sign of the earth element, while Jupiter (5) is in Assistance position. This combination with the three planets at right angles is still beneficial even if they are not in cardinal signs, but less so.

The Special Positions of Lotus *(Patum Kaint)*

Moon in Eleventh   *Or Jupiter in Fourth*
Or Venus in Third   *All lead to growth*

Lotus is the flower of sweet scent and beauty. Certain planets in specified Houses make the person attractive and good at securing support of others, as if he/she is a lotus. They are the Moon (2) in the eleventh (Luck) House, Jupiter (5) in the fourth (Home) House and Venus (6) in the third (Friend) House.

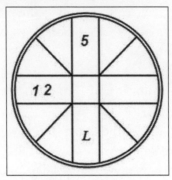

Special combination of the Sun (1), the Moon (2) and Jupiter (5)

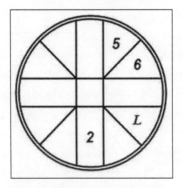

Special Positions of Lotus

The Special Positions of Hardship *(Pintubaat)*
The milder type of hardship:

Fifth is unhappy with Mars,   *Mercury is no fun*
Saturn or Sun   *in Ninth*

Moon and Jupiter suffer in   *And Venus is not great in*
Eighth   *Seventh*

Certain planets in specified Houses make the person face difficulties in something. This depends on the planets and the Houses involved, as well as the Houses of which these planets are Rulers. They are the Sun (1), Mars (3) or Saturn (7) in the fifth (Children) House, Mercury (4) in the ninth (Exaltation) House, the Moon (2) or Jupiter (5) in the eighth (Death) House and Venus (6) in the seventh (Spouse) House.

The risk is higher for the person born on the day of the week with the same number as the planets involved. The day are represented as Sunday (1), Monday (2), Tuesday (3), Wednesday (4), Thursday (5), Friday (6) and Saturday (7). The risk of hardship is much reduced, however, if the planets involved are in Insecure positions or Fall positions.

The stronger type of hardship:

Opposite Lagna with Rahu   *As with Saturn and Mars*
May give hardship to love   *Partners can drift afar*

A more severe hardship is caused by the existence of one or more of the Maleficent planets (Mars (3), Saturn (7) and Rahu (8)) in the seventh (Spouse) House. The person faces risks in marital relationship. The negative side of these planets (violence in the case of Mars (3), somberness and morbidity in the case of Saturn (7) and unrestrained intoxication in the case of Rahu (8)) can pose challenges to marriage. Ketu (9) and Uranus (0) in the seventh (Spouse) House also give the same results but milder.

The hardship caused by the above planets, however, can also be diminished by the influence of Beneficent planets, such as Jupiter (5), if the Beneficent planets are aspected to the planets in hardship (for example, where Jupiter (5) is in trine with that planet).

Rahu in sextile with the Moon

Rahu with Moon in eleventh   *A match not made in heaven*

When the Moon (2) is in the eleventh Houses from Rahu (8) (for example, Rahu (8) in Aries, the Moon (2) in Gemini, which is the eleventh House counted clockwise according to the pattern of transit of Rahu (8)), the Moon (2) affects Rahu (8). The person can have weak unclear judgment. He/she can be self opinionated, or gullible, or easily addicted to gambling and intoxication.

Also, when the Moon (2) is in the third House from Rahu (8) (for example, Rahu (8) in Aries, the Moon (2) is Aquarius, which is the eleventh House counted counterclockwise as in normal transit pattern of other planets), Rahu (8) affects the Moon (2). The person is too soft hearted and too readily answer calls for help from friends and acquaintances. He/she can give low priority to personal grooming, since the Moon (2), the planet of beauty, is clouded by Rahu (8).

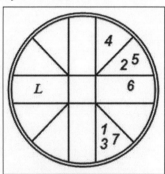

**Special Positions of
mild Hardship**

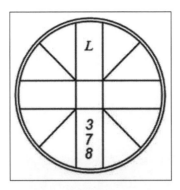

**Special Positions of
strong Hardship**

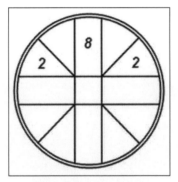

**Rahu (8) in sextile
with the Moon (2)**

The Crescent Moon

The combination of one or more planets in each of the successive Houses is called the Crescent Moon. There must be planets spread over five successive Houses or more. (Some Thai experts believe any planet will do, but others do not allow the counting of Ketu (9) and Uranus (0). This enables all the planets to support each other in turn like a battalion. The person is very successful in high level position, especially in administration or politics. The birth chart of George W Bush is a good example.

The birth chart of George W Bush

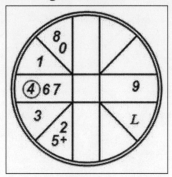

Thai astrology date: Saturday
Calendar Saturday 6 July 1946 at 19.26
Sunrise at 05.55

11. The Special Pairs of Planets

The Friendly Pairs

Jupiter is buddy of the Sun   *The Moon has fun with Mercury*
Venus and Mars are friends   *As again Saturn with Rahu*

Certain pairs of planets enhance each other's good qualities when they are aspected to each other. They are the Sun (1) and Jupiter (5), the Moon (2) and Mercury (4), Mars (3) and Venus (6), Saturn (7) and Rahu (8).

The Sun (1) and Jupiter (5)
The Sun (1) when together with Jupiter (5) enables the person to apply the intelligence of Jupiter (5) to ambition. He/she will make great career achievement. This pair represents power balanced with wisdom.

The Moon (2) and Mercury (4)
The Moon (2) when together with Mercury (4) enables the person to be attractive. He/she is good at dealing with people. This pair is especially good for women, but can make men concentrate too much on romantic charm instead of striving for power. This pair represent the dream comes true, backed by practical action.

Mars (3) and Venus (6)
Mars (3) when together with Venus (6) enables the person to accumulate wealth. But he/she can also be too active in romantic activities because Mars (3) also gives sexual prowess. This pair represents a balanced work life enhanced by wise money knowledge.

Saturn (7) and Rahu (8)

Saturn (7) when together with Rahu (8) enables the person to be a strong group leader. Saturn (7) represents the general public and Rahu (8) power. He/she is successful in mobilizing and controlling friends because of his/her big heart. He/she tends to be lucky in speculation. This pair lessens the bad sides of each other. However, if they are in the seventh (Spouse) House, he/she faces challenges in marriage.

The Enemy Pairs

The Sun punches with Mars   *Rahu spars with Mercury*
Venus dislikes Saturn   *The Moon spurns Jupiter*

Certain pairs of planets diminish each other's good qualities when aspected to each other. They are the Sun (1) and Mars (3), Mercury (4) and Rahu (8), Venus (6) and Saturn (7), the Moon (2) and Jupiter (5). There is an exception, however, in the pair of the Moon (2) and Jupiter (5). Because these two planets are also the Element Pair (earth element), when they are in Taurus, Capricorn or Virgo, which are earth signs, the bad affect is light.

The Sun (1) and Mars (3)

The Sun (1) when together with Mars (3) puts the person at risk of accidents. He/she may do things rashly, without due care or consideration. The risk is both physical and non-physical. He/she should avoid carrying fire arms and always be extra careful driving.

Mercury (4) and Rahu (8)

Rahu (8) when together with Mercury (4) results in difficulties with friends and colleagues. He/she can be too direct and candid, speaking loudly out of turn. He/she may be insensitive and resort to lies which later damage his/her reputation.

Venus (6) and Saturn (7)

Venus (6) when together with Saturn (7) puts the person at risk in love and the management of his/her own wealth.

The Moon (2) and Jupiter (5)

The Moon (2) when together with Jupiter (5) puts the person at risk of arguments with spouse. He/she can marry quite early, or has the risk of a premature relationship, and can have more than one spouse. Such early romance can wear out over time.

The above are the major Enemy Pairs. However, there are other pairs that also have conflicting nature but less harmful as follow:

The Sun (1) with Rahu (8) – the risk of wrong use of power.

Mars (3) with Uranus (0) – the risk of accidents and violence.

Jupiter (5) with Saturn (7) – the risk of discord with elders.

The Element Pairs

Sun and Saturn burn on fire	*Jupiter and Moon swoon on earth*
Mars and Rahu flew in the wind	*Mercury and Venus flush in water*

Planets that are of the same element, when they are aspected to each other, also enhance each other's good quality. They are derived from Taksa, to be explained later, as follow: the Sun (1) and Saturn (7) for fire element, the Moon (2) and Jupiter (5) for earth element, Mars (3) and Rahu (8) for wind element, and Mercury (4) and Venus (6) for water element.

The pairs enhance each other more when they are in the signs of their element; for example, the Sun (1) and Saturn (7) in Aries, Leo or Sagittarius. The affect is at its maximum when they are not only in the signs of their own element but also the cardinal signs, which are the Sun (1) and Saturn (7) in Aries, the Moon (2) and Jupiter (5) in Capricorn, Mars (3) and Rahu (8) in Libra, and Mercury (4) and Venus (6) in Cancer

Their enhancement of each other is somewhat muted, however, if they are in the zodiac signs of the opposite element. For example, the Sun (1) and Saturn (7); the fire pair is muted when it is in Scorpio, a water sign. The opposite of a wind sign is an earth sign.

The Sun (1) and Saturn (7)
The Sun (1) when together with Saturn (7) enables the person to attain goals with more certainty. They can help him/her to accumulate much wealth.

The Moon (2) and Jupiter (5)
Jupiter (5) endows the person with intelligence and academic ability. But it may make the person haughty, aloof and secluded. The Moon (2) makes him/her more charming and aware of others' needs. Hence, success in life is more assured. They can make him/her win easy support for marriage from the parents of spouse, as well as accumulate wealth. This pair is both the Element Pair and the Enemy Pair. In the birth chart, place the weight on the Element Pair. In the transit chart, on the Enemy Pair.

Mars (3) and Rahu (8)
Mars (3) makes the person aggressive, while Rahu (8) makes him/her bold. Together, they make the person a leader because of his/her big heart. But he/she risks having accidents and sudden losses.

Mercury (4) and Venus (6)
Mercury (4) gives the gift of speech. Venus (6) is about sexual pleasure and love of money. Together, the person can accumulate great wealth and tends to be attractive.

The Enhancement Pairs

The Sun is stronger with Venus

Mars' strength increases with Jupiter

The Moon's rush is faster with Rahu

Mercury is brighter with Saturn

Certain planets enhance each other's good quality because they are of opposite nature, meaning that one is a Beneficent planet and the other is a Maleficent planet. They are:

Beneficent planet	Maleficent planet
Venus (6)	The Sun (1)
The Moon (2)	Rahu (8)
Jupiter (5)	Mars (3)
Mercury (4)	Saturn (7)

The Sun (1) and Venus (6)
The Sun (1) gives ambition. Venus (6) gives the love of wealth. Together, they make the person more passionate about achievement.

The Moon (2) and Rahu (8)
The Moon (2) denotes motherhood, while Rahu (8) is the shadow of the earth. He/she can be separated from his/her mother or family at an early age, or may suffer for falling in love or trusting people too easily. He/she will have to help him/herself more than usual, but because the two planets give him/her more endurance, the chance of success is certain. However, he/she can build up a lot of debt, and tends to be somewhat reckless.

Mars (3) and Jupiter (5)
Mars (3) gives courage and is better modified by the intelligence of Jupiter (5). Together, they make the person more determined,

a brilliant strategic thinker, quick at decision making and good at persuasion.

Mercury (4) and Saturn (7)

Mercury (4) gives the gift of speech, but it may err on the side of being too talkative. Saturn (7) gives somberness and seriousness. Together, they make the person successful through technical knowhow and the ability to communicate.

How to read the pairs

For all the pairs of planets as described above, whichever House they are in is augmented by their combined quality. For example, if they are in the eleventh (luck) House, they tend to make the person especially lucky in financial dealings. On the other hand, if they are in a Malefic House, their good power is neutralized.

Planets in strong positions

A Planet is in a strong position and can exert more influence on other planets and on the Houses as follow:

(A) If it is in Ruler position, Exalted position, Perseverance position or Assistance position, or

(B) If it is in a House that has as its Ruler the planet that is its Friendly Pair, its Element Pair or its Enhancement Pair, or

(C) If it is aspected to another planet that is its Friendly Pair, its Element Pair or its Enhancement Pair.

Part IV:

Second Reading of the Birth Chart

12. The Effect of the Planets on Each House and on Each Other

You can now use all the information to the first reading of Princess Diana's chart as follow:

The birth chart of Princess Diana

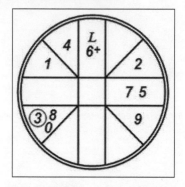

**Thai astrology date: Saturday
Calendar Sunday 2 July 1961 at 01.45**

The first (Self) House is Aries. The Ruler is Mars (3). Mars (3) is in the fifth (Children) House. Having Self in the House of youth gives her a bright young personality; she is fun loving, a joy to be around, looking young and charming. The fifth House is also about sudden luck; therefore, she tends to be showered with gifts and lucky breaks.

The planet representing self in the House related to children makes her own children her main interest. She considers them to represent her and is prepared to spend time and efforts to nurture them, seeing herself as well as her future in them.

Her love and devotion to her children is absolute, and she seeks love and understanding from them in return. She likes being close to children generally, leading to an early job of teaching children.

The fifth House also indicates love. Self in the House related to love makes her sympathetic to any person who shows appreciation and understanding towards her.

Unfortunately, Mars (3) in the fifth House is a Special Position for Hardship. In any person's birth chart, this position can make the person's love tainted somewhat. Self restraint can be weakened even to the point of reputation risk. The fact that Mars (3), a Maleficent planet, is in the House of children causes her children to feel that they also suffer.

The second (Income) House is Taurus. The Ruler is Venus (6). Venus (6) is in the first (Self) House. By having income in the House of self, she is good at finding income. However, Venus (6) is in Insecure position. It can make her income erratic and insecure, or the tendency to overspend, causing occasional financial problems.

In the second (Income) House there is Mercury (4). Mercury (4) is the planet of communication, public relations and diplomacy. Therefore, her income is related to the communication, the promotion and the exhibition of her.

But Mercury (4) is the Ruler of both the third (Friend) House and the sixth (Enemy) House. Friend together with enemy in the House of income makes her too generous with friends who cause her unnecessary spending. It also makes her overspend on social activities. The third (Friend) House also relates to siblings, social contacts and short journeys. By having its Ruler in the House of income, the person's money tends to be spent on such matters.

The third (Friend) House is Gemini. There is the Sun (1) in this House. The Sun (1) is in Assistance position indicating that her friends are people of high society. The Sun (1) is the Ruler of the fifth (Children) House which is also related to enjoyment and pleasure. It therefore gives her the habit of luxury, and the collection of friends that spend money freely.

The Sun (1) in a woman's birth chart also indicates her husband. The Sun (1) in Assistance position makes it easy for her to win the heart of her prospect. It has Ketu (9), the planet of royalty, in the opposite House giving her the chance of marriage to someone in high position.

The fourth (Home) House is Cancer. The Ruler is the Moon (2). The Moon (2) is in the eleventh House, Aquarius in the Special Position of Lotus. The fourth (Home) House is about her father. It indicates a famous, high ranking, well to do father. Unfortunately, the Moon (2), the Ruler of the House related to father, has three Maleficent planets in the opposite House: Mars (3), Rahu (8) and Uranus (0). They pose to him fatal risks regarding illness or accidents.

If you start from the fourth (Home) House, Cancer, which represents her father, then Capricorn is the seventh House from her father. Capricorn therefore represents the spouse of her father. There is Saturn (7) in Capricorn. Saturn (7) in the seventh House is the Special Position of Hardship for Cancer. It indicates the risk of marital difficulty for her father. Saturn (7) in the same House with Jupiter (5), its incompatible pair, also tends to give rise to discord, adding to this risk.

The fifth (Children) House is Leo. It is her most prominent House because it has as many as three planets. The Ruler of Leo is the Sun (1). The Sun (1) is in Assistance position in the third House of society, making her children socially famous. The Sun (1), representing her children, also has Ketu (9), the planet of royalty, opposite. It makes them people of high society.

In this House, Mars (3) is together with Rahu (8), its Element Pair, enhancing the good quality of each other. This pair in the fifth (Children) House makes her children prominent and famous. Rahu (8) is the Ruler of the eleventh (luck) House. Luck in the House of children enables her children to easily find supporters and patrons. Uranus (0) is also a co-Ruler of the eleventh (Luck) House. Its presence in this House also enhances the good effect.

Unfortunately, in this House of children, Mars (3) is in the

Special Position of Hardship. In any birth chart, such a position can make the person's children feel somewhat tainted, and strain the person's relationship with her own children.

In any birth chart, the presence of Rahu (8) in the same House with the Ruler of the first (Self) House (Mars (3)) can open the person to the risk of intoxication, addiction to luxury and incorrect judgment. The fact that Mars (3) is together with Uranus (0) is very important. This is the accident pair.

The presence of Uranus (0) in the same zodiac sign with the Ruler of the first (Self) House of any person normally indicates the following risks:

(A) The person may have incurable illness, or

(B) The person may have to resettle abroad, or

(C) The person may face accidents.

The sixth (Enemy) House is Virgo. Its Ruler is Mercury (4) and it is in the second (Income) House. The sixth House represents problems, obstacles and expenses. All these bad things are brought into the second House by Mercury (4).

The seventh (Spouse) House is Libra. The Ruler is Venus (6) which is in the first (Self) House. Spouse in the House of self indicates a marital success. However, Venus (6) in Insecure position makes marriage insecure.

In all birth charts, Venus (6) is the main indicator of love relationship. In her birth chart, Venus (6) is in trine with its Friendly Pair, Mars (3) in Leo, enhancing the opportunity of romantic success. Mars (3) is especially strong because it is together with Rahu (8), its Element Pair. Venus (6) is also in trine with both Rahu (8), the planet of power, and Ketu (9), the planet of royalty. It indicates the chance of marriage to someone in a high and powerful position. However, Venus (6) has Saturn (7), its Enemy Pair, in Capricorn at right angle. This poses a high risk of marital failure or discord.

The eighth (Death) House is Scorpio. The Ruler is Mars (3). It is in the House of youth, the fifth House. It is also in the Special Position of Hardship. Mars (3) is also the Ruler of the first (Self) House. Self and death in hardship in the House of youth can indicate a risk of death at too young an age.

The ninth (Exaltation) House is Sagittarius. The Ruler is Jupiter (5). It is in the tenth (Career) House. This is the Special Position for Success for Lagna in Aries, a Quadruped sign. It makes her successful in work. This House is also about honor and foreign dealing. Therefore, work related to philanthropy, especially through international organizations or work done in foreign countries which is the characteristic of the ninth (Exaltation) House, makes her more famous. In this House there is Ketu (9). Ketu (9) is especially strong in Sagittarius, therefore, enhancing the impact and the reach of her work to the world.

The tenth (Career) House is Capricorn. The Ruler is Saturn (7) which is in its own House. It makes her work important and long lasting. Saturn (7) being the planet of delay makes her work a heavy burden to her, and the time needed to accomplish her projects long. The combination of Jupiter (5) and Saturn (7) in the same House is not a happy affair. Jupiter (5) is the planet of elders which prefer a reserved lifestyle. Saturn (7) on the other hand is the planet of the common people, preferring a more relaxed lifestyle. Together, she can have difficulty in her relationship with elders.

The eleventh (Luck) House is Aquarius. The three co-Rulers are Saturn (7), Rahu (8) and Uranus (0). Saturn (7) brings luck into the House of career, ensuring success and support. Rahu (8) and Uranus (0) bring luck into the House of children ensuring their success. However, Rahu (8) being in Insecure position in Leo makes luck erratic. In this House there is the Moon (2). It is the Ruler of the fourth (Home) House that also represents father. Father in the House of luck indicates strong support from her father both financially and socially.

Unfortunately, the Moon (2) has Mars (3) in the opposite House. In any birth chart, Mars (3), the planet of courage, in the same House or the opposite House to the Moon (2), tends to make the person take much risk in romances.

The twelfth (Loss) House is Pisces. The Ruler is Jupiter (5) which is in the tenth (Career) House. Jupiter (5) is also in Fall position. It poses the risk of failure, setbacks, negative criticism about her work and her projects.

The effect of the planets on each other and on Lagna can be summarized as follow:

Lagna in conjunction with Venus (6) = the tendency to be easily moved by love, hungry for love, worship love, interested in music, art, luxury and high taste.

Lagna in conjunction with Venus (6) and in sextile with the Moon (2) = charming, well mannered, good looking, well groomed.

Lagna in conjunction with Venus (6) and in sextile with the Sun (1), its Enhancement Pair = the ability to hold herself well, the look of leader, the appearance of knowledge and ability, dexterity.

Lagna in conjunction with Venus (6) and in trine with Mars (3) = bold in showing love, committed to love, not hesitant to love, easy to feel annoyed, short tempered, argumentative.

Lagna in conjunction with Venus (6) and in trine with Rahu (8) = self centered, self adulation, addicted to intoxication, wrong judgment in love, big spender.

Lagna in conjunction with Venus (6) and in trine with Uranus (0) = doing things to be sarcastic or to spite love ones, insensitive to potential criticism about love matters, damage and danger resulting from love.

Lagna in conjunction with Venus (6) and in trine with Ketu (9) = high society person, life with pomp and circumstance, life with ups and downs, self reward, spoiling oneself, taste of luxury.

The Sun (1) in sextile with Mars (3) = life of moving in haste, accident prone, unhappiness from frequent arguments, bold, able to carry out a decisive act.

The Sun (1) in sextile with Rahu (8) = taking risk with illegal actions, risk to reputation, obstacle to success.

The Sun (1) in sextile with Uranus (0) = life full of exciting and unusual events, honor that can be brought down by sudden and unexpected causes.

The Sun (1) opposite Ketu (9) = reputation tremendously enhanced, attainment of top honor, brilliant creative mind.

The Sun (1) in trine with the Moon (2) = life of high society, large circle of friends, likes to show off, proud and not receptive to advice.

The Moon (2) opposite Mars (3) = adventurous in love, attractive and charming, sensitive to love matters, prepared to risk all for love.

The Moon (2) opposite Rahu (8) = enjoying life, intoxication.

The Moon (2) opposite Uranus (0) = self assured, unusual distinctive personality.

The Moon (2) in sextile with Ketu (9) = honorable, moody, too much attention to details, overly sensitive.

Mars (3) in trine with Ketu (9) = striking appearance, descendent of the ruling class, the ability to give command and order.

Mars (3) in conjunction with Rahu (8) = life full of danger, accidents, nocturnal danger (because Rahu (8) is the planet of darkness), when life faces a downturn it can be onerous and beyond repair.

Mars (3) in conjunction with Uranus (0) = impatient, short tempered, prepared to take risks, making ill-planned decisions, accident risk.

Mercury (4) in trine with Saturn (7) = good serious negotiator, intelligent, good at writing.

Mercury (4) in trine with Jupiter (5) = versatile, lucky in negotiation, good at teaching, communication.

Jupiter (5) in conjunction with Saturn (7) = disobedient of elders, disrespectful to elders, lack of support from elders.

Rahu (8) in trine with Ketu (9) = powerful, pervasive influence and impact.

Rahu (8) in conjunction with Uranus (0) = unclear judgment, double crossing, actions that cause scandalous issues to be reopened.

Ketu (9) in trine with Uranus (0) = the ability to revolutionize the social circle, the ability to offer new and untried but successful approaches.

13. Taksa

In Thai astrology, it is important which day of the week is the birth date. Each day of the week is represented by the planets as follow: Sunday – the Sun (1), Monday – the Moon (2), Tuesday – Mars (3), Wednesday – Mercury (4), Thursday – Jupiter (5), Friday – Venus (6) and Saturday – Saturn (7). Each day represents various matters in our lives as follow:

Follower *(Bariwarn)* = your ability to secure help and support from your subordinates, your team, your followers.
Health *(Ahyu)* = how long and how healthy your life can be.
Power *(Dej)* = your ability to command and control.
Success *(Sri)* = your ability to attain honor and high position.
Asset *(Moola)* = your ability to accumulate wealth and assets.
Toil *(Utsaha)* = your work and the efforts and difficulty related to work.
Elder *(Montree)* = support from elders.
Kali = the dark point in your life. The planet that gives you trouble.

The way to identify which planets represent these matters is to go round the format below in the clockwise direction, starting from the number of that day.

1	2	3
6		4
8	5	7

For example, if you are born on Monday, use number 2 as the starting point. The Moon (2) then represents Follower, Mars (3) represents Health, Mercury (4) represents Power, Saturn (7) represents Success, Jupiter (5) represents Asset, Rahu (8) represents Toil, Venus (6) represents Elder and finally the Sun (1) represents Kali.

The only exception is if you are born according to Thai date on Wednesday at night between 18.00 and sunrise the following morning. Instead of starting from number 4 as usual for people born on Wednesday, you have to start from number 8. From number 8 representing Follower, you still go round clockwise to number 6 representing Health, and number 1 representing Power and so on.

The rule of two minuses equal a plus also applies to Taksa. If the planet of Kali occupies the eighth (Death) House or the twelfth (Loss) House, or it is in Insecure position or Fall position, its adverse affect is neutralized. The exception is when it occupies the sixth (Enemy) House. The risk of harm from his/her enemies is still high. If that planet is in Exalted position, the enemies are also more powerful than him/her.

Kali planet can be recovered if it is in Perseverance position. However, in other strong positions (Exalted position, Ruler position and Assistance position) it does not recover. On the contrary, the adverse affect tends to multiply.

Taksa is used as supplementary information. The biggest emphasis is the planet of Kali and the planet of Success. Special attention should be paid to the position of these planets both at birth and later during their transit. Similar to planets, Taksa also transits. The starting point moves one spot each year on your birthday. You can also read Taksa in transit in relation to Taksa at birth. In the year when Success in transit coincides with Success at birth, for example, the person tends to have special luck with speculation and unexpected income. Both types of Taksa charts are available on the website.

14. Nawang Chart

Thai astrology reads the Houses of the planet in relation to each other, instead of reading one planet against the other. The readings do not take into account the exact position of the planets in the zodiac signs. It is broad-brushed, hence easy to use. You can make some general predictions right away. The time window for Lagna staying in a sign is about 2 hours. Even though some planets may change zodiac signs during the 2 hours, it is possible to have a few people with exactly the same birth charts. Are their lives the same? The answer is no. The exact position of the planets within the zodiac signs does matter. It makes the planets stronger or weaker; hence their influences on other planets are different. How is the exact position determined?

Each zodiac sign is 30 degree wide. To narrow down the location, each sign is divided into 9 equal sections called Nawang. Each Nawang covers only 3 degrees and 20 minutes. The degree and minutes show which Nawang the planet is in. For example, a planet position at 2 degrees and 12 minutes is in the first Nawang. The planet position at 4 degrees and 12 minutes is in the second Nawang. Each of the nine Nawangs in a sign is assigned one of the twelve zodiac signs as its Ruler, and this information can be used to plot a Nawang chart. The assignment of the twelve zodiac signs are shown below. For example, if a planet is in the first Nawang of Aries, it is assigned Aries in Nawang chart. In Aries, of course, Mars (3) is the Ruler.

Planets in any of the three fire signs in the birth chart

First Nawang	- Planet assigned is Mars (3)	in Aries
Second Nawang	- Planet assigned is Venus (6)	in Taurus
Third Nawang	- Planet assigned is Mercury (4)	in Gemini
Fourth Nawang	- Planet assigned is the Moon (2)	in Cancer
Fifth Nawang	- Planet assigned is the Sun (1)	in Leo

Sixth Nawang - Planet assigned is Mercury (4) in Virgo
Seventh Nawang - Planet assigned is Venus (6) in Libra
Eighth Nawang - Planet assigned is Mars (3) in Scorpio
Ninth Nawang - Planet assigned is Jupiter (5) in Sagittarius

Planets in any of the three earth signs in the birth chart
First Nawang - Planet assigned is Saturn (7) in Capricorn
Second Nawang - Planet assigned is Rahu (8) in Aquarius
Third Nawang - Planet assigned is Jupiter (5) in Pisces
Fourth Nawang - Planet assigned is Mars (3) in Aries
Fifth Nawang - Planet assigned is Venus (6) in Taurus
Sixth Nawang - Planet assigned is Mercury (4) in Gemini
Seventh Nawang - Planet assigned is the Moon (2) in Cancer
Eighth Nawang - Planet assigned is the Sun (1) in Leo
Ninth Nawang - Planet assigned is Mercury (4) in Virgo

Planets in any of the three wind signs in the birth chart
First Nawang - Planet assigned is Venus (6) in Libra
Second Nawang - Planet assigned is Mars (3) in Scorpio
Third Nawang - Planet assigned is Jupiter (5) in Sagittarius
Fourth Nawang - Planet assigned is Saturn (7) in Capricorn
Fifth Nawang - Planet assigned is Rahu (8) in Aquarius
Sixth Nawang - Planet assigned is Jupiter (5) in Pisces
Seventh Nawang - Planet assigned is Mars (3) in Aries
Eighth Nawang - Planet assigned is Venus (6) in Taurus
Ninth Nawang - Planet assigned is Mercury (4) in Gemini

Planets in any of the three water signs in the birth chart
First Nawang - Planet assigned is the Moon (2) in Cancer
Second Nawang - Planet assigned is the Sun (1) in Leo
Third Nawang - Planet assigned is Mercury (4) in Virgo
Fourth Nawang - Planet assigned is Venus (6) in Libra
Fifth Nawang - Planet assigned is Mars (3) in Scorpio
Sixth Nawang - Planet assigned is Jupiter (5) in Sagittarius

Seventh Nawang	- Planet assigned is Saturn (7)	in Capricorn
Eighth Nawang	- Planet assigned is Rahu (8)	in Aquarius
Ninth Nawang	- Planet assigned is Jupiter (5)	in Pisces

The example of Princess Diana's Nawang chart is shown below (this type of chart is also available from our website). Nawang information is in her planet table in Chapter 1.

Nawang chart of Princess Diana

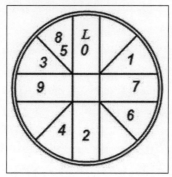

Her Lagna is Nawang Exaltation in Aries, a cardinal sign.

Her Moon (2) is Nawang Exaltation in Libra, a cardinal sign.

Her Saturn (7) is Nawang Exaltation in Capricorn, a cardinal sign.

Her Uranus (0) is Nawang Exaltation in Aries, a cardinal sign.

Certain Nawangs are called Nawang Exaltation (denoted by the letter E in the planet table), meaning that particular planet is especially powerful in its good or bad quality. Not only the planets themselves are powerful, but the Houses of which they are Rulers are also powerful. If it is a Benefic House, the matter related to that House will have a greater chance of success. Even if it is a Malefic House, the matter will still be auspicious, but less.

In Nawang placement, any planet that is assigned the first Nawang in any cardinal sign is automatically in Nawang

Exaltation position (the Moon (2) and Uranus (0) in Diana's chart). Any planet in the birth chart that is in Ruler position, Exalted position and Assistance position that is also in the first Nawang of any sign is also automatically in Nawang Exaltation position (Saturn (7) in Diana's chart).

Similar to the planets, Lagna can also be Nawang Exaltation. Such Lagna helps the person to a generally smooth life without much hardship, able to secure help and assistance from others. This is the case with Princess Diana.

In her example, the Sun (1) in the Nawang chart is in Insecure position, making it weaker than normal, while Mercury (4) is in Exalted position, making it stronger. The strength of the planets in the Nawang chart differentiates the outcome of the birth charts with similar planets.

Part V:

Third Reading of the Birth Chart

The first reading of the birth chart looks at the influence that each House has on other Houses. It reveals the person's priorities in life, the tendency for his/her character development, habits and behaviors – what he/she considers important and what not.

The second reading looks at the influence that each planet has on other planets. Each planet gives its quality, both good and bad, to other planets. The planet interaction, therefore, further modifies habits and behaviors, and also influences the chance of success.

The third reading looks at the likely end results, whether his/her wishes will come true. This is done by reading the planets in relation to Tanu-kaset. This part can make you feel that life events are fatalistic, but it is simply based on statistics gathered over centuries. The best way to use this book is to discover your strengths and weaknesses to improve yourself.

15. Tanu-set and Tanu-kaset

To go into the third reading, you have to understand how to calculate Tanu-set and Tanu-kaset. Tanu-set is the planet in the birth chart that represents your emotions. Tanu-kaset represents the inner self, the innate habit, the real self. Tanu-kaset is the planet in the birth chart that most influences the likely outcome of all matters in your life. Both are available from our website, but can be calculated manually by following these steps, using Princess Diana's birth chart as the example:

The birth chart of Princess Diana

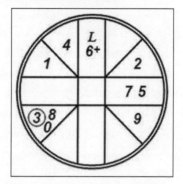

Thai astrology date: Saturday
Calendar Sunday 2 July 1961 at 01.45

(A) See which planet is the Ruler of the first (Self) House. Her Lagna is in Aries. The Ruler of Aries, the first House, is Mars (3).
(B) See which House the planet in A is in. Mars (3) is in Leo.
(C) Count the numbers of Houses counterclockwise, from the House in A to the House in B, starting one at the House in A. The House in A is Aries. The House in B is Leo. Count from Aries to Leo, you get the number of 5.
(D) See which planet is the Ruler of the House in B. The

House in B is Leo. The Ruler of Leo is the Sun (1).

(E) See which House the planet in D is in. The planet in D is the Sun (1). The Sun (1) is in Gemini.

(F) Count the numbers of Houses counterclockwise, from the House in B to the House in E, starting one at the House in B. The House in B is Leo. The House in E is Gemini. Count from Leo to Gemini, you get the number of 11.

(G) Multiply the number in C with the number in F. 5 multiplied by 11 equals 55.

(H) Divide the number in G by 7; see the number that remains. 55 divided by 7 leaves a remainder of 6.

(I) The number in H represents the planet of Tanu-set. The number in H is 6, which is the number of Venus (6). Therefore, Venus (6) is Tanu-set. In the birth chart, a small cross is put beside the planet of Tanu-set.

(J) See which House the planet of Tanu-set is in. Venus (6), Tanu-set, is in Aries.

(K) Tanu-kaset is the planet that is the Ruler of the House where Tanu-set resides. Venus (6), Tanu-set, is in Aries. The Ruler of Aries is Mars (3). Therefore, Mars (3) is Tanu-kaset.

The only exception is when Tanu-set is in Aquarius where there are three Co-Rulers, Saturn (7), Rahu (8) and Uranus (0). Observations have found that the best planet to use for Tanu-kaset is always Saturn (7). To denote Tanu-kaset in the birth chart, a circle is put around the planet of Tanu-kaset.

In operation H, if the remainder is equal to 1 then Tanu-set is the Sun (1), if 2 then Tanu-set is the Moon (2), if 3 then Tanu-set is Mars (3), if 4 then Tanu-set is Mercury (4), if 5 then Tanu-set is Jupiter (5), if 6 then Tanu-set is Venus (6), if 0 then Tanu-set is Saturn (7). Rahu (8), Ketu (9) and Uranus (0) cannot be Tanu-set.

In operation C and F, when the counting involves Rahu (8),

you still count the number going counterclockwise. In operation A and B, if the Ruler is in its own House, then the number in C is 1. Similarly, in operation D and E, if the Ruler is in its own House, then the number in F is 1.

Normally, in the birth chart when the Ruler of any House is in a Malefic House, the matter related to that particular planet tends to be adverse. However, the adversity is neutralized if that planet is Tanu-set.

Reading the Tanu-kaset

Reading the Tanu-kaset is done by using the zodiac sign in which Tanu-kaset occupies as the first (Self) House from Tanu-kaset. The meaning of the first (Self) House is the same as used in the previous readings. Then follow to the next sign counter-clockwise; the next sign is now the second (Income) House from Tanu-kaset. Then to the sign that follows counterclockwise, which is now the third (Friend) House from Tanu-kaset, and so on, until all the twelve Houses from Tanu-kaset have been identified.

The birth chart of Princess Diana

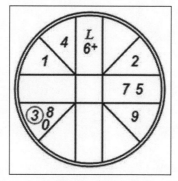

Thai astrology date: Saturday
Calendar Sunday 2 July 1961 at 01.45

Using Princess Diana's birth chart, her Tanu-set is Venus (6), indicated by a small cross, while her Tanu-kaset is Mars (3), and indicated by the circle around the number 3. Mars (3) is in Leo. Suppose you want to read about the likely outcome of her ability to maintain earnings and income in her life, the steps are:

Step 1 Identify which House in relation to Tanu-kaset is about income. It is the second House from Leo, which is Virgo. The Ruler of Virgo, Mercury (4), therefore, is the indicator of the likely outcome to her ability to find income.

Step 2 See where Mercury (4) is in the birth chart. It is in Taurus.

Step 3 Identify which House Taurus is in relation to Lagna. Taurus is the second (Income) House from Lagna.

Step 4 The reading can be done by combining the two meanings. The planet representing income of Tanu-kaset is in the House representing income of self (Lagna). It indicates that the person is able to find and maintain good income throughout her life.

From this point onward, you have to be careful, therefore, when you quote the number of the House, whether it is counted from Lagna or from Tanu-kaset.

16. Special Positions of Tanu-kaset

There are certain planet combinations in relation to Tanu-kaset, and to Lagna, which tend to give certain results. They are listed here for your convenience. Please note that such results, as listed, are also attainable from other planet combinations, but as they are specific to the Houses they are too numerous to list.

The Result in Fame

This combination helps the person to be famous in his/her career. The planet positions are derived from the Special Positions for Success as described in Chapter 10. The conditions for the Result in fame are as follow:

(A) If Lagna is in a Quadruped sign, look at the Ruler of the tenth (Career) House from Lagna. The Result in Fame is when the Ruler of that House is also the planet that is Tanu-kaset. (For example, Lagna is in Aries. The tenth (Career) House from Aries is Capricorn. Saturn (7) is the Ruler of Capricorn. The Result in Fame is when Saturn (7) is Tanu-kaset.)

(B) If Lagna is in a Human sign, look at the Ruler of the first (Self) House where Lagna resides. The Result in Fame is when the Ruler of that House is also the planet that is Tanu-kaset. (For example, Lagna is in Sagittarius. The first (Self) House is Sagittarius. Jupiter (5) is the Ruler of Sagittarius. The Result in Fame is when Jupiter (5) is Tanu-kaset.)

(C) If Lagna is in an Aquatic sign, look at the Ruler of the fourth (Home) House from Lagna. The Result in Fame is when the Ruler of that House is also the planet that is Tanu-kaset. (For example, Lagna is in Pisces. The fourth (Home) House from Pisces is Gemini. Mercury (4) is the

Ruler of Gemini. The Result in Fame is when Mercury (4) is Tanu-kaset.)

(D) If Lagna is in Scorpio, look at the Ruler of the seventh (Spouse) House from Lagna. The Result in Fame is when the Ruler of that House is also the planet that is Tanu-kaset. (For example, Lagna is in Scorpio. The seventh (Spouse) House from Leo is Taurus. Venus (6) is the Ruler of Taurus. The Result in Fame is when Venus (6) is Tanu-kaset.)

Saturn (7) in the tenth (Career) House from Tanu-kaset can present difficulty in maintaining fame. Initial success can fade away later, except when Saturn (7) is also in Capricorn or Aquarius where it is in Ruler positions. On the other hand, the presence of the Sun (1), the Moon (2) or Jupiter (5) in the tenth (Career) House from Tanu-kaset enables the person to maintain fame for life. Mars (3) in the tenth (Career) House from Tanu-kaset indicates a struggle before fame.

The Result in High Leadership *(Aek Kaint)*
This combination helps the person to develop strong leadership ability. It occurs when there are the Sun (1), the Moon (2) and Mercury (4) in conjunction with Lagna, or with Tanu-kaset. The absence of the Moon (2) still gives the same affect, but less.

The Result in High Ability *(Pet Song Sode)*
This combination helps the person to acquire high technical ability and achieve high career position. It occurs when:

(A) The planet that is Tanu-set is in conjunction with the planet that is Tanu-kaset, <u>or</u>

(B) The planet that is Tanu-set is the same planet that is Tanu-kaset.

The effect of B) is stronger than A), and it is further enhanced if Lagna is also in conjunction with the above, or the planets involved are aspected to Lagna. Success is more assured if the Sun (1) is also aspected to the planets.

The Result in High Position *(Paya Mantaturaj)*

This combination helps the person to the highest and most powerful career position, especially in big organizations. It occurs when:

(A) All three planets that are related to self, Tanu, occupy the same House; they are Lagna (or the Ruler of the first (Self) House from Lagna) and Tanu-set and Tanu-kaset, <u>and</u>

(B) The Sun (1) also occupies that House, <u>and</u>

(C) The Sun (1) is strong in Ruler position or Exalted position or Perseverance position or Assistance position.

The result is still good if there are only two conditions, A) and B), above, but to a lesser extent.

Three examples are shown below:

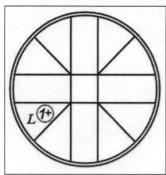 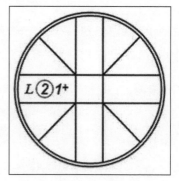

In the first drawing, the Sun (1) is in Ruler position and it is both Tanu-set and Tanu-kaset.

In the second drawing, the Sun (1) is Tanu-set and in Perseverance position. The Moon (2) is Tanu-kaset.

In the third drawing, the Sun (1) is in Exalted position. Venus (6) is Tanu-set and Mars (3) is Tanu-kaset.

The Result in High Exaltation *(Supataman)*

This combination helps the person gain technical knowledge and management ability for career advancement, particularly in civil service, and success in foreign dealings. It occurs when:

(A) The planet that is the Ruler of the ninth (Exaltation) House from Lagna is also the planet that is Tanu-kaset, <u>or</u>

(B) The planet that is the Ruler of the ninth (Exaltation) House from Tanu-kaset is also the planet that is Tanu-kaset, <u>or</u>

(C) The planet that is the Ruler of the ninth (Exaltation) House from Tanu-kaset is in conjunction with Lagna.

Three examples are shown here:

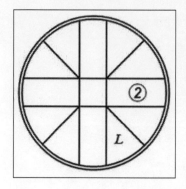
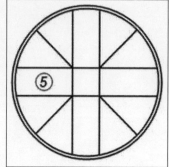

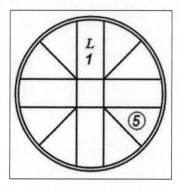

In the first drawing, Lagna is in Scorpio. The ninth (Exaltation) House from Lagna is Cancer. The Ruler of Cancer is the Moon (2). The Result of High Exaltation is when the Moon (2) is also Tanu-kaset.

In the second drawing, Tanu-kaset is Jupiter (5) in Cancer. The ninth (Exaltation) House from Tanu-kaset in Cancer is Pisces. The Ruler of Pisces is Jupiter (5). The Result of High Exaltation is when Jupiter (5) is also Tanu-kaset.

In the third drawing, Tanu-kaset is Jupiter (5) in Sagittarius. The ninth (Exaltation) House from Tanu-kaset in Sagittarius is Leo. The Ruler of Leo is the Sun (1). The Result of High Exaltation is when the Sun (1) is in conjunction with Lagna.

The Result in High Achievement *(Uttataman)*

This combination helps the person succeed in education and career similar to the Result in High Exaltation. It occurs when:

(A) The planet that is the Ruler of the House where Tanu-kaset (Ruler of Tanu-kaset) occupies is in the ninth (Exaltation) House from Tanu-kaset, or

(B) The planet that is the Ruler of the House where Lagna occupies (Ruler of Lagna) is in the ninth (Exaltation) House from Lagna together with Tanu-kaset.

Two examples are shown here:

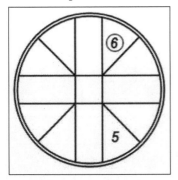 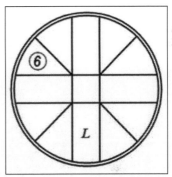

In the first drawing, Tanu-kaset Venus (6) is in Pisces. The Ruler of Pisces is Jupiter (5) which is in Scorpio, the ninth (Exaltation) House from Tanu-kaset.

In the second drawing, Lagna is in Libra. The Ruler of Libra is Venus (6) which is in Gemini, the ninth (Exaltation) House from Lagna.

The Result in High Luck *(Lapasarava)*

This combination gives the person skill in winning support and lucky breaks from others, enabling him/her to accumulate wealth. It occurs when:

(A) The planet that is the Ruler of the second (Income) House from Lagna is in the eleventh (Luck) House from Tanu-kaset, <u>or</u>

(B) The planet that is the Ruler of the second (Income) House from Tanu-kaset is in the eleventh (Luck) House from Lagna, <u>or</u>

(C) The planet that is the Ruler of the eleventh (Luck) House from Lagna is in the eleventh (Luck) House from Tanu-kaset, <u>or</u>

(D) The planet that is the Ruler of the eleventh (Luck) House from Tanu-kaset is in the eleventh (Luck) House from Lagna.

These four cases are shown here:

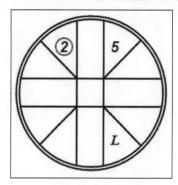 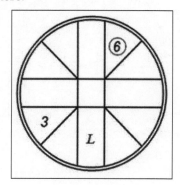

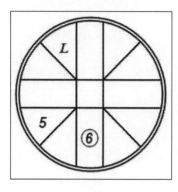 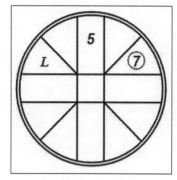

In the first drawing, the second (Income) House from Lagna is Sagittarius. The Ruler of Sagittarius is Jupiter (5) which is in Pisces. Pisces is the eleventh (Luck) House from Tanu-kaset which is the Moon (2) in Taurus.

In the second drawing to the right, Tanu-kaset is Venus (6). The second (Income) House from Tanu-kaset is Aries. The Ruler of Aries is Mars (3) which is in Leo, the eleventh (Luck) House from Lagna.

In the third drawing, the eleventh (Luck) House from Lagna is Pisces. The Ruler of Pisces is Jupiter (5) which is in Leo. Leo is the eleventh (Luck) House from Tanu-kaset, which is Venus (6) in Libra.

In the fourth drawing, Tanu-kaset is Saturn (7) in Aquarius. The eleventh (Luck) House from Tanu-kaset is Sagittarius. The Ruler of Sagittarius is Jupiter (5) which is in Aries, the eleventh (Luck) House from Lagna.

The Result of High Luck can also be obtained when the planet that is the Ruler of the second (Income) House from Tanu-kaset, or the planet that is the Ruler of the eleventh (Luck) House from Tanu-kaset, is in conjunction with Tanu-kaset.

17. The Tendency for Wealth

Wealth, money and income can come from four sources: work, inheritance, marriage and lucky speculation. Wealth and income are indicated by the following Houses from Lagna and from Tanu-kaset:

The first (Self) House – meaning one must be healthy and with the right frame of mind.

The second (Income) House – how secured the source of income.

The fourth (Home) House – the ability to hold properties.

The fifth (Children) House – the ability to attract luck and gains from speculation.

The seventh (Spouse) House – the support of spouse or business partners.

The ninth (Exaltation) House – the support of elders or money earned from career position.

The eleventh (Luck) House – the support of colleagues.

When the Ruler of any of these Houses is in Ruler position, Exalted position, Enhancement position or Assistance position, the planet is strong, giving higher chance of financial success. The same applies if it is together with its Friendly Pair, Element Pair or Enhancement Pair, or if the Ruler of one of these Houses is in another House in the group listed above, with the Ruler of that particular House also back in the House of the first planet. For example, the Ruler of the first (Self) House is in the second (Income) House while the Ruler of the second (Income) House is back in the first (Self) House. The position swap can also be a threesome or more. The best effect is when the Houses involved are the first (Self) House, the second (Income) House and the eleventh (Luck) House.

You also have to examine the Ruler of the second (Income)

House from Tanu-kaset and the Ruler of the eleventh (Luck) House from Tanu-kaset. If the planets are strong and occupy a House from Lagna that is related to wealth, then success is greater. The most important Houses related to wealth are the second (Income) House and the eleventh (Luck) House.

The best indication of wealth earned by the person him/herself is to have Jupiter (5), the planet of good judgment, or Venus (6), the planet of money skill, in good aspect (in conjunction with, in trine with, etc.) to the Ruler of the second (Income) House from Tanu-kaset or the Ruler of the eleventh (Luck) House from Tanu-kaset. For the person that gains wealth from inheritance, the Rulers of the fourth (Home) House from Tanu-kaset and the eighth (Death) House from Tanu-kaset are normally in strong position. Wealth from marriage is normally indicated by a strong Ruler of the seventh (Spouse) House from Tanu-kaset that resides in the second (Income) House or the eleventh (Luck) House from Tanu-kaset. A strong Ruler of the fifth (Children) House from Tanu-kaset can indicate wealth from speculation if it occupies the second (Income) House or the eleventh (Luck) House from Tanu-kaset, especially if it is Rahu (8), the planet of taking chances.

The birth chart that has a planet in the same zodiac sign of the same element as that planet (for example, either the Sun (1) or Saturn (7) or both, the Fire Element Pair, in Aries, Leo or Sagittarius, the Fire Element Signs) also make the person successful financially. The best is when the birth chart has all such four elements.

The poor possibility for wealth is normally indicated by the position of the Ruler of the second (Income) House from Lagna either

(A) being in a Malefic House from Lagna, or
(B) it is weak in Insecure position or Fall position.

It is also indicated in the following conditions in relation to Tanu-kaset:

(A) When the Ruler of the second (Income) House from Tanu-kaset is in a Malefic House from Lagna, or

(B) It is weak in Insecure position or Fall position, or

(C) When there is a planet in Fall position in the second (Income) House from Tanu-kaset, or

(D) When the Ruler of a Malefic House from Tanu-kaset is in the second (Income) House from Tanu-kaset, especially the Ruler of the twelfth (Loss) House from Tanu-kaset.

That person should be very cautious about finance.

18. Successes in Love

Challenges to love may arise in the following situations:

(A) The Ruler of the seventh (Spouse) House from Lagna is in a Malefic House, or

(B) The Ruler of the seventh (Spouse) House from Lagna is in the House that has its Enemy Pair as the Ruler, or in a House together with a planet that is its Enemy Pair, or

(C) Venus (6), the planet of love, is aspected by a Maleficent planet, especially Saturn (7) its Enemy Pair, or

(D) There is Mars (3), Saturn (7), Rahu (8), Ketu (9) or Uranus (0) in the seventh (Spouse) House from Lagna.

In relation to Tanu-kaset, the Ruler of the seventh (Spouse) House from Tanu-kaset in a Benefic House from Lagna tends to indicate a successful love life. The opposite is when the Ruler of the seventh (Spouse) House from Tanu-kaset is in conjunction with the Ruler of a Malefic House from Tanu-kaset. The presence of the planets in D) above in the seventh (Spouse) House from Tanu-kaset also present challenges, but milder.

Please note that the above conditions on their own may not be conclusive, because the relevant planets can be saved by having good aspect with Jupiter (5) or if they are Rulers in their own Houses, or by being in conjunction with its Friendly Pair, Element Pair or otherwise.

The positions of Lagna in the birth charts of the man and the birth chart of the woman can also indicate a successful marriage. These conditions are not exclusive, however. Successful marriage can also be indicated by many other conditions. They are:

(A) When Lagna in the man's birth chart is in the same zodiac sign with the woman's Lagna, or in the sign opposite the Lagna in the woman's birth chart (for example, the man's Lagna is in Virgo and the woman's in Pisces), <u>or</u>

(B) When Lagna in the man's birth chart is in the third (Friend) House, or the fifth (Children) House, or the ninth (Exaltation) House, or the eleventh (Luck) House from Lagna in the birth chart of the woman, <u>or</u>

(C) When the Ruler of the first (Self) House from Lagna in the man's birth chart is in the first (Self) House, the second (Income) House or the eleventh (Luck) House from Lagna in the birth chart of the woman, and vice versa with the woman in the birth chart of the man.

19. Successes in Education

Education is indicated by Mercury (4) and Jupiter (5). Either or both in the first (Self) House of Lagna or in the fifth (Children) House and the ninth (Exaltation) House from Lagna make the person devoted to study. If these two planets are aspected to each other (for example, in conjunction or in trine to each other), the person is quick at absorbing new knowledge and skill.

If the Ruler of the ninth (Exaltation) House from Lagna is in a strong position, and is well aspected to Lagna and to the Sun (1), the planet of honor, success in higher education is enhanced.

The pair of Mercury (4) and the Sun (1) in the same House is also called the Knowledge Pair. The person is well educated, unless the two are within 3 degrees of each other when Mercury (4) is blinded by the brightness of the Sun (1). He/she has to put in extra effort and time.

In relation to Tanu-kaset, the supreme success in education can be seen when Jupiter (5) is strong in Pisces (Ruler), Gemini (Insecure), Cancer (Exalted), Virgo (Insecure) and Sagittarius (Ruler), and also in the position to influence Tanu-kaset (in conjunction with, opposite to, etc.).

20. The Tendency for Good Health

The tendency for good health starts with the first (Self) House from Lagna. If its Ruler is in a strong position, the person is healthy and has positive outlook to life. He/she looks after him/herself well. But the Ruler of the first (Self) House from Lagna should also be in a Benefic House. If it is in the eighth (Death) House from Lagna, the person tends to be physically weak. The same applies if it aspected by Maleficent planets, especially in the opposite House or a House at right angle. In term of health, the Moon (2) is as important as Lagna. Therefore, the above mentioned conditions with regard to Lagna also apply to the position of the Moon (2).

The risk of accident or chronic illness is high in the following conditions:

(A) The Ruler of the first (Self) House from Lagna is together with Uranus (0) in the sixth (Enemy) House or the eighth (Death) House from Lagna, or

(B) The Ruler of the first (Self) House from Lagna is together with its Enemy Pair in the House where its Ruler is the Sun (1), Mars (3) or Saturn (7), or

(C) Lagna is clamped by Maleficent planets, in the second House and the twelfth House from Lagna, or

(D) The Ruler of the first (Self) House from Lagna is clamped by Maleficent planets, in the second House and the twelfth House counted from the House where that Ruler occupies.

Please note that the above conditions on their own may not be conclusive, because the relevant planets can still be saved by having good aspect with Jupiter (5). However, the person should emphasize healthy habits and be cautious in travel.

21. The Third Reading

You can now combine all the above information for the final reading. We again use the example of Princess Diana's chart as follows:

The birth chart of Princess Diana

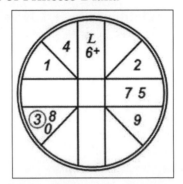

Thai astrology day: Saturday
Calendar Sunday 2 July 1961 at 01.45

Self

Her Lagna is in Nawang Exaltation. It makes her overall life comfortable and free of struggles. It also indicates that she will outshine, be more important and make greater achievement than everybody in her family.

Venus (6) is Tanu-set and it is in Aries.

Venus (6) as Tanu-set makes her interested in fashion, parties, enjoyment, gala events and luxury. Ketu (9), the planet of royalty, is in trine with both Venus (6) and Lagna, which makes her want to appear regal, refined and majestic. But this habit is costly, and can adversely affect her finances as indicated by Venus (6) being in Insecure position.

Venus (6) is in Aries. The Ruler of Aries is Mars (3). Therefore Mars (3) is Tanu-kaset and it is in Leo. In relation to Tanu-kaset

(Mars (3) in Leo) the ninth (Exaltation) House is Aries. The Ruler of Aries is Mars (3). Therefore Mars (3) also represents exaltation and honor.

Mars (3) is in Leo, which is the fifth (Children) House from Lagna. Having the planet that represents exaltation and honor in the House that is related to luck, fame and youth indicates the achievement of fame and recognition at a young age. She is also successful with her own children, gets pregnant easily and experiences easy child birth. The more children she has, the more fame and attention she receives. It also indicates that her children will be famous.

In relation to Tanu-kaset (Mars (3) in Leo) the fifth (Children) House is Sagittarius. In Sagittarius there is Ketu (9), the planet of royalty. This indicates that her children will also be the upper class, the royalty.

Love

In relation to Tanu-kaset (Mars (3) in Leo) the seventh (Spouse) House is Aquarius. The Ruler of Aquarius is both Rahu (8) and Saturn (7). Therefore, both Rahu (8) and Saturn (7) represent her spouse.

Rahu (8) is an Asian symbol for a giant, or a powerful person, reflecting the social position of her husband. Saturn (7) is the planet of age, making her willing to accept an older husband.

Saturn (7), representing spouse, is in the tenth (career) House from Lagna, which is also the House related to work and obligation. Having the planet that represents spouse in the House related to obligation indicates the possibility of a marriage out of obligation to her family.

Saturn (7), representing spouse, is together with Jupiter (5), the planet of elders, which also indicates that the marriage might be arranged by her elder relatives.

Uranus (0) is another co-Ruler of Aquarius, and therefore, also represents spouse. Both Rahu (8) and Uranus (0) are in Leo, the fifth (Children) House from Lagna. Having spouse in the House of youth leads her into an early marriage.

In relation to Tanu-kaset (Mars (3) in Leo) the twelfth (Loss) House is Cancer. Its Ruler is the Moon (2). Therefore, the Moon (2) represents loss and separation. The Moon (2) is in Aquarius. Aquarius is the seventh (Spouse) House from Tanu-kaset, representing spouse. Having the planet that represents loss and failure in the House of spouse poses a big risk to her marriage.

The Moon (2) is the planet of romance, and in her chart it is especially strong because it is in Nawang Exaltation position. Mars (3), on the other hand, is the planet that makes the person courageous, but can be too daring and carefree, and Mars (3) is the key to this person's life, being Tanu-kaset. The Moon (2) is opposite to Mars (3), so they can directly influence each other. The planet that represents a strong desire for romance is influenced by the planet that represents a daring self. The pair is potentially troublesome.

Venus (6) has Saturn (7), its Enemy Pair, at right angle. Saturn is particularly powerful, being both the Ruler in its own House as well as in Nawang Exaltation position. Saturn (7) exerts its influence on Venus (6), the planet of love, resulting in difficulty.

Work

She is famous from her work. This is because in relation to Tanu-kaset (Mars (3) in Leo) the ninth (Exaltation) House is Aries. The Ruler of Aries is Mars (3). Mars (3) being Tanu-kaset gives the Result in High Position.

Her work is indicated by the tenth (Career) House from Lagna which is Capricorn. There are two planets in there, Jupiter (5) and Saturn (7). Jupiter (5) is especially auspicious. Jupiter (5) is the Ruler of Sagittarius. Sagittarius is the fifth (Children) House from Tanu-kaset (Mars (3) in Leo). Having Jupiter (5) representing children in the House of career indicates that her work is related to children; working for foundations to improve their welfare, lifting their living standards.

From Lagna in Aries, a Quadruped sign, Jupiter (5) in the tenth House is the Special Position for Success. This makes her work especially successful. However, Jupiter (5) is also the Ruler of Pisces, the eighth (Death) House from Tanu-kaset. Jupiter (5) is also in Fall position. Having the planet that represents death in the House of career indicates that her work may not reach the summit.

Saturn (7) is the Ruler of the sixth (Enemy) House from Tanu-kaset. The planet that represents enemy is in the House of career, causing opposition and obstacles in work. Saturn (7) in Capricorn is also the Ruler in its own House, hence powerful, making the difficulties more severe.

Jupiter (5) represents people of higher authority, while Saturn (7) represents the followers. Although they are not arc enemies, they do not get along well. The pair makes it difficult for her to seek help from elders.

The tenth (Career) House from Tanu-kaset is Taurus with Venus (6) as the Ruler. Venus (6) is in Aries but in Insecure position. Therefore, her work is intermittent and faces a few disruptions. It can, over time, wear down her resolves and cause her projects to eventually close down.

Finance

Both the Ruler of the second (Income) House and the Ruler of the eleventh (Luck) House from Tanu-kaset are Mercury (4). Mercury (4) is in Taurus, the second (Income) House of Lagna. Having the planet representing luck in the House of income enables her to find good income.

The Ruler of the first (Self) House from Tanu-kaset is the Sun (1). Therefore the Sun (1) also represents self. It is in the third (Friend) House from Lagna. It is especially strong because it is in Assistance position and has Ketu (9), the planet of royalty, directly opposite. Having the planet that represents self in the

House of friend helps her to attain social acclaim and recognition. It indicates that she can seek more help from friends than from elder people in high position.

Mercury (4) is the planet of speech and advertising. Having Mercury (4) as the Ruler of the House related to income and luck indicates that her source of income is linked to speeches, communication or her exposure to the media.

Accident

Her birth chart has several indications of accident or illness:

(A) She is born on a Saturday according to Thai astrology. In Taksa, the planet that represents health and longevity is Jupiter (5). It is in Fall position, indicating the first risk.

(B) Jupiter (5), the indicator of Health by Taksa, is in conjunction with Saturn (7). Saturn (7) is the Ruler of Capricorn, the sixth (Enemy) House from Tanu-kaset. Health being together with enemy is the second risk.

(C) Saturn (7) is especially strong because it is in its own House, and also in Nawang Exaltation, therefore the risk is higher than normal.

(D) The Ruler of the first (Self) House from Lagna is Mars (3). It is under pressure by being in conjunction with the planet of destruction, Uranus (0). Mars (3) and Uranus (0) are the pair with accidents. Uranus (0) in her chart is also particularly strong, being in Nawang Exaltation.

(E) The fourth (Home) House from Tanu-kaset is Scorpio. This House is also about vehicle. Its Ruler is also Mars (3) which is in the fifth (Children) House of Lagna. Mars (3) in the fifth House is a Special Position of Hardship. Having the planet representing vehicle in a hardship position indicates high risks regarding travelling.

(F) Mars (3), the planet that represents self, is reached by two Maleficent planets, Rahu (8) and Uranus (0).

Part VI:

Predicting the Future

22. How to Read the Planets in Transit

In Astrology, one would do very well just to be accurate in the readings of the birth charts alone. The birth charts can predict the overall direction of your life. To read the events year by year, however, is much more difficult. Each planet affects all other planets, both in the positions at birth and in their transit positions. The effect caused by one planet may be negative, and offset by another planet that is positive. Also, it may be easy to read about a major event, a once in a lifetime affair, or the potential change in political position that starts and ends on fixed dates. The smaller events tend to be quite difficult to read.

Furthermore, the interpretation requires the exact knowledge of the circumstances that you face. No one knows this as well as you. Therefore, when you consult a professional astrologer, you may still be frustrated by the imprecise answers and advices given. This alone is the reason why many people take up astrology: to interpret the information by themselves.

The effect of planets in transit on the Houses

The first basic principle is that when a planet transits into a House, it brings the matter related to itself to that House. The matter related to the transiting planet is determined by which House in the birth chart that planet is the Ruler of, and which House in the birth chart that planet occupies.

For example, suppose Jupiter (5) is the Ruler of the ninth (Exaltation) House in the birth chart, or Jupiter (5) occupies the ninth (Exaltation) House in the birth chart. When Jupiter (5) transits into the tenth (Career) House, it can bring exaltation, promotion, and new honor to the person's career. Of course, this is not conclusive because there are all other planets to consider also. If Jupiter (5) is the Ruler of one of the Malefic Houses in the birth chart, or occupies one of those Houses, the effect is the opposite.

The first (Self) House in transit *(Kaljak)*

The second principle is the first (Self) House in transit, which is denoted in the transit chart as @.

In this principle, the first (Self) House is deemed to move counterclockwise from one zodiac sign to the next. The transit time of the @, the first (Self) House in transit, through each zodiac sign, varies according to a set table, and may last 2-11 years for each sign. During those 2-11 years, you can also consider that particular sign to be the first (Self) House to which the matters related to all other Houses are referenced to.

The change of the first (Self) House in transit from one sign to another occurs on the birthday of the relevant year as set out in the table. When the table determines that @ is in a particular sign (say, from 5 to 7 years of age), then the change occurs on the day following the date that the person completes his/her 4 years, and lasts until the date that the person completes his/her 7 years. The first (Self) House in transit that covers any specified date for each person is available on the website.

The steps to reading the planets in transit in relation to @, the first (Self) House in transit, are as follows:

First: Examine the birth chart in relation to @

For an event to occur, the possibility must first be hinted by the planets at the time of birth. The positions of the planets at birth of course remain fixed. Their aspect to each other (being in conjunction or trine with each other, etc) may already support the event to happen at one point in the person's lifetime; for example, the chance of the person becoming the President of a country.

But when?

The key is in @, the first (Self) House in transit. When the person's age is 1, @ is in the first (Self) House with Lagna. But no person can become President at age 1.

In later years, @ moves counterclockwise from one sign to

another; from the first House from Lagna to the second House from Lagna, then to the third House from Lagan, and so on. Until @ reaches the House where everything fits in, relative to the planet positions at birth, then all the jigsaw pieces would fall into place for the event to happen. It will occur only while @ is in that House, not before and not after.

To examine whether or not that possibility is hinted in the birth chart, you just remove Lagna from the birth chart, leaving all other planets in place. Then use @, the first (Self) House in transit, as Lagna, and read the planets at birth in relation to @ as Lagna.

For the event related to career success, you look to both the ninth (Exaltation) House from @ and the tenth (Career) House from @, and read the positions of the planets at birth. If the planets related to those Houses are strong, then this is the first hint.

For easy memory, the first step can be summarized as **'Natal planets vs. @'**.

Second: Examine the planets in transit relative to Lagna.

For the event to occur, it will also be hinted by the planets in transit relative to Lagna. The planets in transit must be auspicious (or for a bad event, detrimental) to Lagna. Basically, you ignore all the planet positions in the birth chart, leaving only Lagna. Then put in the planets in transit.

For an event of career success, for example, the auspicious planets in transit must be in the position to reach Lagna (being in conjunction or trine with Lagna, etc., or in a Benefic House from Lagna, such as the eleventh (Luck) House, etc.).

But which planets?

The planets to be used for the examination are the Rulers of the relevant Houses in relation to @.

This can be clearly explained as follow:

Step 1 You start by first identifying the House that is related to the issue that you want to read, and it's Ruler. This is done relatively to @.

For example, suppose you want to read the matters related to the person's career for this year. Suppose this year @, the first (Self) House in transit, is in Aries. Look to the Ruler of Capricorn, which is the tenth House from @ in Aries. The Ruler of Capricorn is Saturn (7). Therefore while @ is in Aries, Saturn (7) represents career.

Step 2 See in which zodiac sign Saturn (7) in transit is. Suppose Saturn (7) in transit is in Libra. It is very strong in its Exaltation position. This is the first hint from the planets in transit that while @ is in Aries and Saturn (7) is in Libra, the person's career is especially strong.

Step 3 Identify which House in relation to Lagna Libra is. Suppose Lagna is in Aquarius. In relation to Lagna, Libra is the ninth (Exaltation) House. Then, having Saturn (7) in transit, representing career, in the House of exaltation is another strong indication.

We can read that while @ is in Aries, the person tends to find special success with his/her career when Saturn (7) is in Libra, the House of honor.

Step 4 You have to examine all other Houses, in relation to @ in Aries, which may be related to the person's career advancement. For example, the ninth (Exaltation) House from @, which is Sagittarius. The Ruler of Sagittarius is Jupiter (5). See where Jupiter (5) in transit is in relation to Lagna and read it like Saturn (7) in step 3.

For career advancement, the other Houses that should be examined include:

- the Ruler of the House where (@) occupies (Aries) because it shows the ability of self,

- the Ruler of the fourth (Home) House from @ (Cancer) if it involves elders and relatives,

- the Ruler of the fifth (Children) House from @ (Leo) and the eleventh (Luck) House from @ (Aquarius) if it involves luck and support from others, etc.

You have to look at all the planets because of their different transit time. In this example, Saturn (7) is in a zodiac sign for as long as 2 and a half years; therefore, it is not a good indicator of the event that may occur in one single month and not in other months. To narrow down the time window to months and weeks, or even days, the 'small' planets which move fast must be read all together. In addition, you have to look at the minus signs that may be hinted from the Malefic Houses in relation to @ as well.

For easy memory, the second step can be summarized as **'House Rulers from @ vs. Lagna'**.

<u>Third: Examine the planets in transit relative to @</u>

Further indications must be examined for planets in transit relative to @, the first (Self) House in transit. The planets in transit must be auspicious (or for a bad event, detrimental) to @.

For a good indication of career success, for example, the auspicious planets in transit must be in the positions to reach @ (being in conjunction or trine with @, etc., or in a Benefic House from @, such as the eleventh (Luck) House, etc.).

But, again, which planets?

The planets to be used in the third examination are the planets at birth, in the birth chart. You simply take away Lagna and put @ into the birth chart, and then see which House in relation to @ the planets occupy. For example, if the Sun (1) is in the second (Income) House from @, then the Sun (1) represents income.

This can be clearly explained as follows:

<u>Step 5</u> In this example, we are still enquiring about the person's career while @ is in Aries. Therefore, relative to @ in Aries, the Houses relevant to Career are the ninth House and the tenth House from Aries. They are Sagittarius and Capricorn.

In the birth chart, suppose in Sagittarius there is Jupiter (5). Therefore, while @ is in Aries, Jupiter (5) in transit represents honor, the ninth House from Aries. Suppose also that in the birth chart in Capricorn there is Venus (6). While @ is in Aries, Venus (6) in transit represents career.

Step 6 Look at the transit chart to see where Jupiter (5) in transit is. Suppose it is in Aquarius. Identify which House in relation to @ Aquarius is. Aquarius is the eleventh (Luck) House from @ in Aries. The planet in transit that represents honor is now in the House (relative to @) that represents luck. This is another indication of success.

You then do the same exercise for Venus (6). Suppose Venus (6) is in conjunction with @ in Aries, this is another success indicator.

You then have to examine all other planets in the birth chart that occupy both Benefic Houses and Malefic Houses from @ in order to gather all the indications, plus and minus. If all the indicators are pluses, then a conclusion can be easily made. However, when the indicators are mixed, you have to evaluate and weigh each indicator for the net result. Sometimes the presence of a minus indicator can mean that the eventual result may still be successful but faces an initial delay, or the result may turn out to be less than expected.

For easy memory, the third step can be summarized as **'Natal Planets from @ vs. @'**.

The technique above reads the Houses against @ and does not take into account the exact position of the planets in the House. Is it too broad-brushed? Do people with exactly the same birth charts face the same events? The answer is yes, but the height of achievement and the depth of crisis is not the same. It depends on the strength of the planets as shown in the Nawang chart, detail of which is too complicated for this book. However, you will see from the readings of famous people that the technique is still effective.

The planets in transit in Princess Diana's chart
We can apply the above principles to Princess Diana's major life

events. In this example, the planets in transit are underlined in order not to confuse them with planets in the birth chart.

<u>Parental separation</u>

Date 1 April 1967

The birth chart of Princess Diana

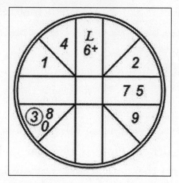

Thai astrology date: Saturday
Calendar Sunday 2 July 1961 at 01.45

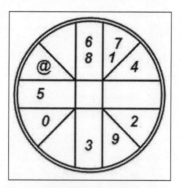

Chart of planets in transit
on 1 April 1967

<u>The planets in transit in relation to Lagna and to the Houses</u>

The first indication is made by <u>Jupiter (5) in transit</u>. It is in Cancer, opposite to Saturn (7) in the birth chart. The two planets reach each other. Jupiter (5) is the planet of elders, while Saturn (7) is the planet of difficulties. Their aspect to each other indicates

158

difficulties caused to her by elders during that time. Saturn (7) in transit in Pisces is also in sextile with Jupiter (5) in the birth chart. They also reach each other confirming the difficulties.

Rahu (8) in transit, the planet of change, is in Aries. It is in conjunction with Lagna in the birth chart. Having the planet that represents change reaching self indicates a big change in life about to occur.

Rahu (8) in transit is in trine with Uranus (0) in transit in Leo. Uranus (0) is the planet of sudden and adverse change. The two reaching each other indicates that the change is sudden and adverse.

Uranus (0) in transit is in Leo, in conjunction with Mars (3) in the birth chart. In the birth chart, Mars (3) the Ruler of the first (Self) House. Having the planet that represents sudden and adverse change reaching self in the birth chart is another indication.

Uranus (0) in transit in Leo is also in conjunction with Rahu (8), the planet of change, in the birth chart. Again, the aspect of these two planets indicates a sudden and disruptive change about to come.

The planets in the birth chart in relation to the first (Self) House in transit

Her age is 6. Between the ages of 5 and 7, her first (Self) House in transit, denoted by @, is in Gemini.

The House that represents father for the woman is the fourth House. In relation to @ in Gemini, the fourth (Home) House, counted counterclockwise from Gemini, is Virgo. The Ruler of Virgo is Mercury (4). Therefore while @ is in Gemini, Mercury (4) represents father.

In the birth chart, Mercury (4) is in Taurus. In relation to @ in Gemini (the first (Self) House in transit), Taurus is the twelfth (Loss) House. Having the planet that represents father in the House that now represents loss is the first risk.

The House that represents mother for the woman is both the ninth House and the tenth House. Here, the risk is more clearly indicated by the tenth House. In relation to @ in Gemini, the tenth House is Pisces. The Ruler of Pisces is Jupiter (5). Therefore, while @ is in Gemini, Jupiter (5) represents mother.

In the birth chart, Jupiter (5) is in Capricorn. In relation to @ in Gemini, Capricorn is the eighth (Death) House. Having the planet that represents mother in the House that now represents death and separation is the second risk.

The House that represents happiness in the family is the ninth House. In relation to @ in Gemini, the ninth House is Aquarius. The Co-Rulers of Aquarius are Rahu (8) and Uranus (0). Therefore, while @ is in Gemini, both Rahu (8) and Uranus (0) represent family happiness.

In the birth chart, both Rahu (8) and Uranus (0) are in Leo, and both are in Insecure position. Both planets that represent family happiness are in weak positions, a risk to family harmony.

<u>The planets in transit in relation to the first (Self) House in transit</u>

In relation to @ in Gemini, the Ruler of the fourth House and the Ruler of the tenth House that represent the father and the mother are Mercury (4) and Jupiter (5). Therefore, while @ is in Gemini, Mercury (4) represents father and Jupiter (5) represents mother.

<u>Jupiter (5) in transit</u> is in Cancer, while <u>Mercury (4) in transit</u> is in Aquarius. In relation to <u>Jupiter (5) in transit</u>, <u>Mercury (4) in transit</u> is in the eighth (Death) House from Cancer. While in relation to <u>Mercury (4) in transit</u>, <u>Jupiter (5) in transit</u> is in the sixth (Enemy) House from Aquarius. Both planets are, therefore, in a Malefic House of each other. The planet representing father is in the House of death of the mother. And the planet representing mother is in the House of enemy of the father. This is a big risk.

In relation to @ in Gemini, the Houses that represents mother are the ninth (Exaltation) House which is Aquarius, and the tenth

(Career) House which is Pisces. Here, the indication is clearer in Pisces than Aquarius. While @ is in Gemini, Pisces represents the House of mother.

In the transit chart, <u>Saturn (7) in transit</u> is in Pisces. In relation to @ in Gemini, Saturn (7) is the Ruler of the eighth (Death) House. Therefore, while @ is in Gemini, Saturn (7) represents death. Having the planet that represents death and separation in the House of mother is the final risk.

<u>Her marriage</u>
Date 29 July 1981
The birth chart of Princess Diana

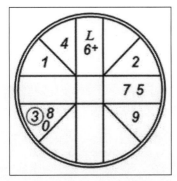

Thai astrology date: Saturday
Calendar Sunday 2 July 1961 at 01.45

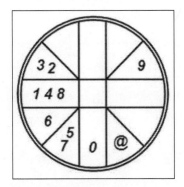

Chart of planets in transit on 29 July 1981

<u>The planets in transit in relation to Lagna and to the Houses</u>

In relation to Lagna, the seventh (Spouse) House is Libra. The Ruler of Libra is Venus (6). <u>Venus (6) in transit</u> is in Leo, in conjunction with Mars (3), the Ruler of the first (Self) House from Lagna. The planet that represents spouse reaches the planet representing self, the first indication of possible marriage. <u>Venus (6)</u> is with its Friendly Pair, Mars (3), enhancing the chance of success.

<u>Venus (6) in transit</u> is also in conjunction with Rahu (8) in the birth chart, the planet of change. The planet that represents spouse reaches the planet of change, indicating the possible change to marital status.

<u>The planets in the birth chart in relation to the first (Self) House in transit</u>

Her age is 21. Between the ages of 21 and 28, her first (Self) House in transit, denoted by @, is in Scorpio.

In relation to @ in Scorpio, the seventh House is Taurus. In the birth chart there is Mercury (4) in Taurus. Therefore, while @ is in Scorpio, Mercury (4) represents spouse.

In the transit chart, <u>Mercury (4) in transit</u> is in Cancer. In relation to @ in Scorpio, Cancer is the ninth (Exaltation) House. The planet that represents spouse is in the House of family happiness and honor is the third indication.

<u>The planets in transit in relation to the first (Self) House in transit</u>

In relation to @ in Scorpio, the seventh (Spouse) House is Taurus. The Ruler of Taurus is Venus (6). Therefore while @ is in Scorpio, Venus (6) represents spouse.

In the transit chart, <u>Venus (6) in transit</u> is in Leo. In relation to Lagna, Leo is the fifth (Children) House. The planet that represents spouse is in the House of sudden luck and fame is another indication.

In the transit chart, Taurus, the House that now represents

spouse, is in trine with Jupiter (5) in transit and Saturn (7) in transit in Virgo.

In relation to @ in Scorpio, Jupiter (5) is the Ruler of the second (Income) House and the fifth (Children) House, and Saturn (7) is the Ruler of the third (Friend) House. Therefore, while @ is in Scorpio, Jupiter (5) represents wealth and fame (in addition to children), and Saturn (7) represents friend.

The planets in transit that represent wealth, sudden luck and friend can reach the House of spouse. This is another indication of a possible marriage to a friend that brings wealth and fame to her.

Taurus, the House that represents spouse, is also in sextile with Rahu (8) in transit, the planet of change, indicating a possible change to the marital status.

Her first son
Date 21 June 1982
The birth chart of Princess Diana

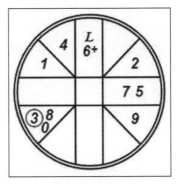

Thai astrology date: Saturday
Calendar Sunday 2 July 1961 at 01.45

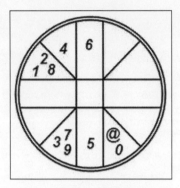

**Chart of planets in transit
on 22 June 1982**

The planets in transit in relation to Lagna and to the Houses

The Ruler of the fifth (Children) House from Lagna in the birth chart is the Sun (1). Therefore, the Sun (1) represents child-birth. Rahu (8) in transit is in Gemini, in conjunction with the Sun (1) in the birth chart. The planet of change reaching the planet that represents childbirth is the first indication.

The planets in transit in relation to the first (Self) House in transit

Her age is still 21; therefore, her first (Self) House in transit, denoted by @, is still in Scorpio.

In relation to @ in Scorpio, the House related to children is Pisces. The Ruler of Pisces is Jupiter (5). Therefore, while @ is in Scorpio, Jupiter (5) represents children.

Jupiter (5) in transit is in Libra. It is opposite to Lagna. The planet that represents children can reach self (Lagna) is the second indication.

In relation to @ in Scorpio, Mars (3) is the Ruler of the first (Self) House. Therefore, while @ is in Scorpio, Mars (3) represents self.

In the transit chart, Mars (3) in transit is in Virgo. It is opposite to Pisces, the House that now represents children. The planet that represents self reaching the House that represents children is another indication.

In relation to @ in Scorpio, Virgo is the eleventh (Luck) House. Mercury (4) is the Ruler of Virgo. Therefore, while @ is in Scorpio, Mercury (4) represents luck.

In the transit chart, Pisces, the House that now represents children, is in sextile with <u>Mercury (4) in transit</u>. The planet that represents luck can reach the House that represents children is the final indication.

<u>Her second son</u>
Date 15 February 1984
The birth chart of Princess Diana

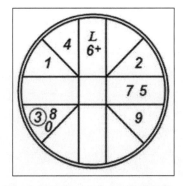

Thai astrology date: Saturday
Calendar Sunday 2 July 1961at 01.45

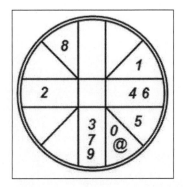

Chart of planets in transit on 15 February 1984

The planets in transit in relation to Lagna and to the Houses

In the birth chart, the fifth (Children) House from Lagna is Leo. In Leo there is Mars (3). Therefore, Mars (3) represents children. In the transit chart, Mars (3) in transit is in Libra. It is opposite to Lagna. The planet in transit that represents children reaching self (Lagna) is the first indication.

The planets in transit in relation to the first (Self) House in transit

Her age is 23; therefore, her first (Self) House in transit, denoted by @, is still in Scorpio.

In relation to @ in Scorpio, the House related to children is still Pisces. The Ruler of Pisces is Jupiter (5). Therefore, during this period, Jupiter (5) still represents children.

In the transit chart, Jupiter (5) in transit is in Sagittarius. It is in trine with Lagna in the birth chart. The planet that represents children reaching self (Lagna) is another indication. Jupiter (5) in transit is also strong because it is the Ruler in its own House. In relation to Lagna, the ninth (Exaltation) House is Sagittarius. Sagittarius is, therefore, in the House related to family happiness. The planet that represents children is in the House of family happiness, another indication.

<u>Her own divorce</u>

Date 15 July 1996

The birth chart of Princess Diana

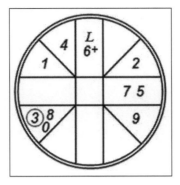

Thai astrology date: Saturday
Calendar Sunday 2 July 1961at 01.45

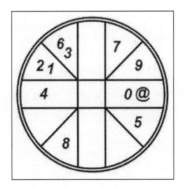

Chart of planets in transit
on 15 July 1996

<u>The planets in transit in relation to Lagna and to the Houses</u>

In relation to Lagna, the eleventh (Luck) House is Aquarius. The Ruler of the eleventh (Luck) House is Rahu (8). Therefore, Rahu (8) represents luck. In the transit chart, <u>Rahu (8) in transit</u> is in Virgo. In relation to Lagna, Virgo is the sixth (Enemy) House. The planet that represents luck is now in the House of enemy.

In relation to Lagna, Mercury (4) is the Ruler of Virgo, the sixth (Enemy) House. Therefore, Mercury (4) represents enemy. In the transit chart, <u>Mercury (4) in transit</u> is in Cancer which is the fourth (Home) House from Lagna. The planet that represents enemy is in the House of home.

<u>The planets in the birth chart in relation to the first (Self) House in transit</u>

Her age is 36. Between the age of 32 and 36, her first (Self) House in transit, denoted by @, is in Capricorn.

While @ is in Capricorn, it is in conjunction with Saturn (7) in the birth chart, the planet of sorrow. Therefore, while @ is in Capricorn, there is a risk of her having to face issues that appears to her quite heavy and permanent (because Saturn (7) is strong, being the Ruler in its own House).

In the birth chart, @ is also in conjunction with Jupiter (5), the Ruler of Pisces. In relation to @ in Capricorn, Pisces is the third House that is related to society. While @ is in Capricorn, Jupiter (5), therefore, represents friends and society. In the birth chart, Jupiter (5) is in Fall position. Therefore, while @ is in Capricorn, her social status risks being damaged by the Fall position of Jupiter (5).

In relation to @ in Capricorn, Jupiter (5) is also the Ruler of Sagittarius, which is the twelfth House. This is the House of loss, failure, disruption, double dealing and secrecy. While @ is in Capricorn, therefore, Jupiter (5) also represents all these bad qualities. Having @, the first (Self) House in transit in conjunction with Jupiter (5) in the birth chart is like having all the bad qualities introduced to self.

Finally, Jupiter (5) and Saturn (7) are the incompatible pair of planets. The first (Self) House in transit, @, is in conjunction with these two planets in the birth chart, which is another hint.

The planets in transit in relation to the first (Self) House in transit

In relation to @ in Capricorn, the seventh (Spouse) House is Cancer. Therefore, while @ is in Capricorn, Cancer represents spouse. In the transit chart, Cancer is aspected by many Maleficent planets all at once.

It is in sextile on the one side with Mars (3) in transit in Taurus, and on the other side with Rahu (8) in transit in Virgo. It also has Uranus (0) in transit in Capricorn, the opposite House. It is also in trine with Saturn (7) in transit in Pisces. Many Maleficent planets in transit are able to reach the House of spouse, indicating substantial risks.

The planets in transit, Mars (3), Rahu (8) and Uranus (0) are particularly harmful because in the birth chart they are in Leo, which in relation to @ in Capricorn is now the eighth (Death) House. Therefore, while @ is in Capricorn, all these three planets represent death and separation.

In relation to @ in Capricorn, Virgo is the ninth (Exaltation) House. Therefore, while @ is in Capricorn, Virgo represents family happiness and honor. In the birth chart, Rahu (8) is in Leo. In relation to @ in Capricorn, Leo is now the eighth House of death. Therefore while @ is in Capricorn, Rahu (8) brings with it the element of death.

In the transit chart, Rahu (8) in transit is in Virgo. The planet that represents death is in the House that now represents family happiness and honor, which is the final risk.

Her death

Date 31 August 1997

The birth chart of Princess Diana

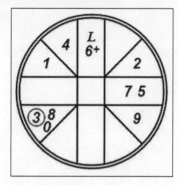

Thai astrology date: Saturday
Calendar Sunday 2 July 1961at 01.45

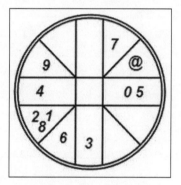

Chart of planets in transit
on 31 August 1997
Thai astrology date: 1 September 1997

The planets in transit in relation to the Houses

None of the indicators shown in this book are ever conclusive enough, whether on their own or together with others, to accurately foretell death. They are only indicators of risks.

To look for major risks in life, you have to first observe the 'big' planets, which are Jupiter (5), Saturn (7), Rahu (8) and

Uranus (0). You have to see their transit positions in relation to Lagna, in relation to their original positions in the birth chart, and in relation to @, the first (Self) House in transit.

The other planets, which are considered 'small', move through all the 12 zodiac signs within one year, or only slightly longer. They do so every year, therefore, they are not good indicators of risks that may happen only once in a lifetime.

The first indicator of a major risk is when these 'big' planets in transit are able to reach their original positions, or reach the original positions of other 'big' planets, in the birth chart.

In the transit chart, <u>Saturn (7) in transit</u> in Pisces is in sextile with Jupiter (5) in the birth chart, in Capricorn. <u>Jupiter (5) in transit</u> is also in Capricorn, in conjunction with Saturn (7) in the birth chart.

The two planets in the transit chart have reached their incompatible pairs in the birth chart, indicating a big risk about to happen.

Furthermore, <u>Rahu (8) in transit</u> is in Leo, in conjunction with both Rahu (8) and Uranus (0) in the birth chart. A Maleficent planet in transit reaching other Maleficent planets in the birth chart is a big risk.

Finally, <u>Uranus (0) in transit</u> is in Capricorn, also in conjunction with both Jupiter (5) and Saturn (7) in the birth chart. Uranus (0), the planet of sudden calamity, has reached the incompatible pair of planets in the birth chart.

All these show the high probability of a major risk building up and about to break out. It only waits for the 'small' planets to add their weights to raise the probability to the maximum.

<u>The planets in the birth chart in relation to the first (Self) House in transit</u>

Her age is 37. Between the age of 37 and 39, her first (Self) House in transit, denoted by @, is in Aquarius.

To start with, while @ is in Aquarius, there are already indications of difficulties in the birth chart.

In the birth chart, in Leo, opposite to Aquarius, there are three Maleficent planets, Mars (3), Rahu (8) and Uranus (0). Being opposite to @, they can exert their bad influences directly on @, now the House of self. The risk is present as long as @ is in Aquarius.

In the birth chart, in Aquarius there is the Moon (2). The Moon (2) is the Ruler of Cancer. In relation to @ in Aquarius, Cancer is its sixth (Enemy) House. While @ is in Aquarius, the Moon (2) represents enemy. Self in transit, @, is therefore in conjunction with the planet in the birth chart that now represents its enemy. This is the second risk.

The planets in transit in relation to the first (Self) House in transit

The final indicators are as follow:

(A) The House related to short journeys and close friends is the third House. In relation to @ in Aquarius, the third (Friend) House is Aries. In the birth chart, there is Venus (6) in Aries. Therefore, while @ is in Aquarius, Venus (6) represents a short journey and close friend. In the transit chart, Venus (6) in transit is in Virgo. In relation to @ in Aquarius, Virgo is the eighth (Death) House. The planet that represents a friend and short journey is in the House that now represents death. It indicates the risk of accident in a short journey with a friend.

(B) The House related to vehicle is the fourth House. In relation to @ in Aquarius, the fourth (Home) House is Taurus. In the birth chart, there is Mercury (4) in Taurus. Therefore, while @ is in Aquarius, Mercury (4) represents vehicle. In the transit chart, Mercury (4) in transit is in Cancer. In relation to @ in Aquarius, Cancer is the sixth (Enemy) House. The planet that represents vehicle in the House that now represents enemy. This adds to the risk of vehicle accident.

(C) In the transit chart, the <u>Sun (1) in transit</u> is in Leo. It is in conjunction with Mars (3) in the birth chart, its accident pair. This is the final risk.

In this example, you can see that with the benefit of hindsight it is much easier to explain the events in the past in relation to the planets. It is of course more difficult to determine exactly the things that may happen in the future.

Part VII:

Birth Charts of Famous People

23. Birth Charts of Famous People

Prince Charles

We believe this to be the birth chart of Charles the Prince of Wales, born on Sunday 14 November 1948 at 21.14 in London, United Kingdom, GMT+00.00. He was married on 29 July 1981 and had two sons in 1982 and 1984. He was officially separated from his spouse in 1992 and officially divorced in 1996.

We have not obtained official verification of the birth time; therefore, cannot claim without any doubt that it is his birth chart.

The birth chart of Prince Charles

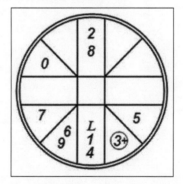

Thai astrology date: Sunday
Calendar Monday 15 November 1948 at 04.14
Sunrise at 06.18

Self

Lagna in Libra indicates a man of justice, jovial, sociable, and careful with his speech, likes harmony and his social circle.

Venus (6) is the Ruler of the first (Self) House. It is in Virgo, the twelfth (Loss) House. Fortunately, it is in Fall position, minimizing the damage. It being in the House of Loss tends to make him cautious, careful, and able to see through others' intentions; he likes to work behind the scenes, and does not advertise his intelligence.

Mars (3) is Tanu-set. The person with Mars (3) as Tanu-set can be somewhat moody, easy to lose temper, retains his simmering anger for a long time. It can also make the person wanting to clear personal differences without delay, with a serious outlook to most life matters.

Mars (3) is also Tanu-kaset. The same planet as Tanu-set and Tanu-kaset is the Result in High Ability. It makes him hard working, determined and serious; a man of high standards who meticulously guards against mistake.

Mars (3) in Scorpio is also strong in Ruler position, giving him endurance, the ability to hide his feelings, carrying the look of shouldering a big burden. He always feels busy solving problems, a life without the trivial.

In relation to Tanu-kaset (Mars (3) in Scorpio), the sixth (Enemy) House is Aries. Its Ruler is Mars (3). It is in Scorpio, the second (Income) House from Lagna. It indicates the tendency for expenses, outflows and difficulties related to money matters. Fortunately, Mars (3) is Tanu-set, making the adverse effect less damaging.

In relation to Tanu-kaset (Mars (3) in Scorpio), the fourth (Home) House is Aquarius. Saturn (7) is the Co-Ruler of Aquarius. Saturn (7) is in Leo, which is the eleventh (Luck) House from Lagna.

The fourth House of a man's birth chart represents his mother. The planet that represent mother is in the House of luck and in the Special Position of Plenty for people with Lagna in Libra, a Human sign. It indicates luck and support from his mother. Saturn (7) is also the planet of strength, endurance and longevity, the characteristics of his mother. Saturn (7) is the planet of fire element. In Leo, a fire sign, it is especially strong.

In relation to Tanu-kaset (Mars (3) in Scorpio), the fifth (Children) House is Pisces. The Ruler of Pisces is Jupiter (5).

Jupiter (5) is in Sagittarius, strong in Ruler position and also in Special Position of Plenty for people with Lagna in Libra, a Human sign.

It indicates that his son is in high social echelons. His son will also rule. This is hinted by Jupiter (5) being followed by a string of planets that are related to royalty, Mars (3), the Sun (1) and Ketu (9).

Love

In relation to Tanu-kaset (Mars (3) in Scorpio), the seventh (Spouse) House is Taurus. The Ruler of Taurus is Venus (6) which is in Virgo. This is the twelfth (Loss) House from Lagna. Venus (6) in Virgo is also in Fall position. This is a negative indication about love life.

The planet that represents marriage, love and spouse is in the House of Loss and in Fall position. There are risks of difficulty, loss of honor and diminishing love associated with such planets. No matter how high love starts off, it risks deteriorating over time, becoming less valuable, less respectable.

The seventh (Spouse) House, Taurus, is also clamped by Maleficent planets, Rahu (8) and Uranus (0) on either side, and another Maleficent planet, Mars (3), opposite. This poses high risks of separation and divorce.

In relation to Tanu-kaset (Mars (3) in Scorpio), the fourth (Home) House is Aquarius. Its Ruler is Rahu (8), which is in Aries. Unfortunately, Rahu (8) in the seventh (Spouse) House from Lagna is the Special Position of Hardship, reconfirming the risk of divorce.

The fourth House of a man's birth chart represents his mother. The planet representing mother is in the House that represents spouse and is in hardship position. It indicates the possibility of discord between the mother and the spouse.

His first marriage
The birth chart of Prince Charles

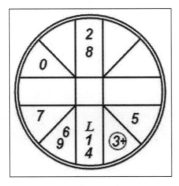

Thai astrology date: Sunday
Calendar Monday 15 November 1948 at 04.14

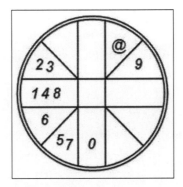

Chart of planets in transit
on 29 July 1981

His first marriage occurs at the age of 33. Between the ages of 33 and 39, the first (Self) House in transit, @, is in Pisces.

In the birth chart, in relation to @ in Pisces, Virgo is the seventh (Spouse) House. There is Venus (6) in that House. The planet of love is opposite and able to reach self, @.

In relation to @ in Pisces, the Ruler of the first (Self) House is Jupiter (5). Therefore, while @ is in Pisces, Jupiter (5) represents self. In the transit chart, Jupiter (5) is in Virgo, the seventh

179

(Spouse) House from @. The planet in transit that represents self in the House that represents spouse is another indication.

Venus (6) in the birth chart is in the seventh (Spouse) House from @ in Pisces. Therefore, while @ is in Pisces, Venus (6) represents spouse. In the transit chart, Venus (6) is in Leo, and Leo is the eleventh (Luck) House from Lagna. The planet in transit that represents spouse in the House that represents luck also indicates that the first marriage will happen as planned although it will face difficulties later

Is the second marriage long lasting?

When a person has more than one spouse, the first spouse is represented by the seventh (Spouse) House from Tanu-kaset. The first spouse is, therefore, Taurus. The Ruler of Taurus is Venus (6). In the birth chart, Venus (6) is in the House of loss in relation to Lagna, and in Fall position, indicating a possible failure.

The House that represents the second wife is the next one from Taurus, counting counterclockwise. It is Gemini. The Ruler of Gemini is Mercury (4). Mercury (4) is in conjunction with Lagna. The planet that represents the second spouse together with self indicates a happy union.

Mercury (4) in conjunction with Lagna is also the Special Position of Plenty for people with Lagna in Libra, a Human sign. This makes Mercury (4) strong. Mercury (4) is also clamped by three planets that represent royalty, Mars (3) on one side, Ketu (9) on the other side, and the Sun (1) in the middle.

It indicates that the second spouse will become Queen.

His reign

This man is born to rule. There are several indications in the birth chart.

(A) The Sun (1) in conjunction with Lagna in Libra is the Special Position for Success for people with Lagna in Libra, a Human sign.

(B) In relation to Tanu-kaset, Mars (3) in Scorpio, the tenth
(Career) House is Leo. The Ruler of Leo is the Sun (1),
which is in conjunction with Lagna. The planet that
represents career reaches self, and is also in Special
Position, indicating that he will attain a high position, be
a leader.

(C) In relation to Tanu-kaset, Mars (3) in Scorpio, the eighth
(Death) House is Gemini. The Ruler of Gemini is
Mercury (4). Mercury (4) is in conjunction with Lagna,
also the Special Position of Plenty for people with Lagna
in Libra, a Human sign. The planet that represents death
also reaches self, and is also in Special position,
indicating that he will receive great inheritance.

(D) In relation to Tanu-kaset, Mars (3) in Scorpio, the ninth
(Exaltation) House is Cancer. The Ruler of Cancer is the
Moon (2), which is in Aries opposite Lagna and also very
strong in Perseverance position. Having the planet that
represents honor able to reach self is another indication.

(E) The four planets that are related to royalty, the Sun (1),
Mars (3), Jupiter (5) and Ketu (9) are on either side or
in conjunction with both versions of self, Lagna and
Tanu-kaset, a high probability that he becomes a king.

This book is written in 2009. Based on the planet positions that
can be calculated in advance, we believe that if the birth time is
correct he will be King in 2014, at the age of 66.

The birth chart of Prince Charles

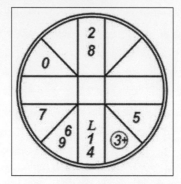

Thai astrology date: Sunday
Calendar Monday 15 November 1948 at 04.14

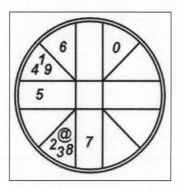

Chart of planets in transit
on 5 July 2014

Between the ages of 64 and 68, the first (Self) House in transit, @, is in Virgo.

The first indication is shown in the birth chart. In relation to @ in Virgo, the ninth (Exaltation) House is Taurus. The Ruler of Taurus is Venus (6). While @ is in Virgo, therefore, Venus (6) represents honor. In the birth chart, Venus (6) is in Virgo. @ is in conjunction with Venus (6). Self in transit reaches the planet that represents honor.

Venus (6) in conjunction with @ is also the Special Position of

Plenty for people with Lagna or @ in Virgo, a Human sign. This makes Venus (6) the planet representing honor especially strong.

In relation to @ in Virgo, the fourth (Home) House is Sagittarius. In the birth chart, Jupiter (5) is in Ruler position in Sagittarius. Jupiter (5) in the fourth House is the Special Position of Lotus and the Special Position of Plenty while @ is in Virgo, a Human sign. It indicates special height of achievement while @ is in Virgo.

In the transit chart, we can narrow down the period to July 2014. In that month, Jupiter (5), the planet of double Special Positions while @ is in Virgo, transits into Cancer. In relation to Lagna in Libra, Cancer is the tenth (Career) House. In relation to @ in Virgo, Cancer is the eleventh (Luck) House. Jupiter in Cancer is also especially strong in Exalted position. The planet of special success and luck in the House related to career and luck is a firm indication.

In relation to @ in Virgo, the eighth (Death) House is Aries. Its Ruler is Mars (3). In the birth chart, Mars (3) in Scorpio is strong in Ruler position and is in sextile with @. Therefore, while @ is in Virgo, major things related to death can occur to him.

In the transit chart, Mars (3), now the planet of death, is in Virgo, in conjunction with @. Mars (3) in Virgo is especially strong in Perseverance position. It indicates a significant inheritance.

In relation to @ in Virgo, the second (Income) House is Libra, and the ninth (Exaltation) House is Taurus. Venus (6) is the Ruler of both Houses. Therefore, while @ is in Virgo, Venus (6) represents both money and honor.

In the transit chart, Venus (6) in Taurus is strong in Ruler position. Taurus is the ninth (Exaltation) House in relation to @. The planet in transit that represents money and honor is in the House of honor, another strong indication.

Finally, in relation to @ in Virgo, the first (Self) House is Virgo, and the tenth (Career) House is Gemini. Mercury (4) is the

Ruler of both Houses. Therefore, while @ is in Virgo, Mercury (4) represents both self and career.

In the transit chart, Mercury (4) is in Gemini, strong in Ruler position. Gemini is the tenth (Career) House in relation to @. The planet in transit that represents self and career is now in the House of career. In this House there is also Ketu (9), the planet of royalty, in transit. In that month, royalty reaches career.

We, therefore, see his ascension occurring between the 1 July and 17 July 2014.

Prince William

We believe this to be the birth chart of Prince William, born on Monday 21 June 1982 at 21.03 in London, United Kingdom, British Summer Time, GMT+01.00. He graduated in 2006 and received appointment, decoration and titles in 1982, 2002 and 2008. His mother passed away on 31August 1997.

We have not obtained official verification of the birth time, therefore, cannot claim without any doubt that this is his birth chart.

The birth chart of Prince William

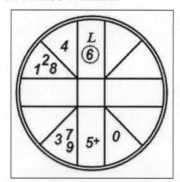

Thai astrology date: Monday
Calendar Tuesday 22 June 1982 at 03.03
Sunrise at 05.52

Self

Lagna in Aries indicates an agile person who loves freedom; he is strong built, hard headed, open and straightforward, sincere, courageous, daring, prepared to give and take and a man with a big heart.

The Ruler of the first (Self) House is Mars (3). It is in Virgo, the sixth (Enemy) House from Lagna.

Mars (3) is in Enhancement position, making the person enthusiastic, ambitious, diligent, determined, and prepared to struggle and fight for his beliefs. However, having self in the House of enemy indicates the risk of opposition, problems and obstacles in the way. His work can generate enemies, and heavy burden.

Jupiter (5) is Tanu-set, giving him the tendency of intellectual capacity, policy making, love of justice and a good sense to rule.

Venus (6) in Aries is Tanu-kaset. It indicates a peace loving gentle person; one who promotes group spirit, avoids controversies, encouraging compromise among friends. It also gives him the gift of wealth, the love of art and antiquities, the mellow feeling. It makes him easily touched and torn in search for love.

Venus (6), Tanu-kaset, is in conjunction with Lagna. This makes him want to be a leader, prepared to stand out, to volunteer, to command, to give orders and to show his mettle.

Jupiter (5), the planet of honor, opposite both versions of self indicates that his life will be dedicated to helping the less fortunate, doing honorable charitable work, both within his own country and abroad.

In relation to Tanu-kaset, Venus (6) in Aries, the fifth (Children) House is Leo. Its Ruler is the Sun (1) which is in Assistance position in Gemini. It indicates a person who is famous from an early age.

The Sun (1), representing his children, is also especially strong. It is strengthened by the Enhancement Pair (the Moon (2) and Rahu (8)). Rahu (8) is the Ruler of the eleventh (Luck) House.

It also has Jupiter (5) in trine. Jupiter (5) is the Friendly Pair of the Sun (1) and is the Ruler of the ninth (Exaltation) House. All this indicates that he will bear children who will also rule.

This man is also born to rule, indicated in the birth chart as follow:

(A) Mars (3) in the sixth House from Lagna is the Special Position of Plenty. He is successful in work.

(B) The Ruler of the ninth (Exaltation) House from Tanu-kaset is Jupiter (5). Jupiter (5) is in Libra, opposite to Lagna. Exaltation can reach self.

(C) In Virgo also there is Ketu (9), the planet of royalty, together with Mars (3), the Ruler of the first (Self) House. Having royalty together with self enhances the chance to rule.

(D) The Sun (1) in Gemini is in sextile with both Lagna and with Venus (6), Tanu-kaset. All four planets related to royalty, the Sun (1), Mars (3), Jupiter (5) and Ketu (9) therefore can influence the three versions of self, a strong indication that he will become king.

His mother

For a man, the House related to mother is the fourth (Home) House. In relation to Tanu-kaset (Venus (6) in Aries), the fourth (Home) House is Cancer. The Ruler of Cancer is the Moon (2). It is in Gemini, in conjunction with the Sun (1) which is strong in Assistance position.

The Moon (2), the planet of beauty, as the Ruler of the fourth House indicates an attractive mother. The planet of mother is with a strong Sun (1), the planet of father, indicates that his mother's status will be lifted by marriage.

The Moon (2) is also with its Enhancement Pair, Rahu (8). It indicates a mother who is famous worldwide. All these three planets in Gemini have Jupiter (5) in trine.

Jupiter (5) is the Ruler of Sagittarius. In relation to Tanu-kaset, Venus (6) in Aries, Sagittarius is the ninth (Exaltation) House. The planet that represents honor can reach these planets, indicating parents of high social standing.

Since Cancer is the House related to his mother, we can also read the risk associated with his mother's life by using Cancer as the first (Self) House representing his mother.

If we do so, then the eighth House from Cancer is Aquarius. Aquarius is, therefore, the House of death related to his mother. Rahu (8), the Ruler of Aquarius, can therefore indicate the risk of death to his mother. Rahu (8), representing death, is in conjunction with the Moon (2), the planet representing mother, indicates a risk.

Furthermore, if we do so, then the eleventh House of loss from Cancer is Gemini. Gemini is, therefore, the House of loss related to his mother. The Moon (2), the planet representing mother, is in the House of loss, another indication of risk to his mother.

The hint of complication to his mother's marriage can also be seen. If we use Cancer as the first (Self) House of his mother, the seventh (Spouse) is Capricorn. The Ruler of Capricorn is Saturn (7). There are three Maleficent planets reaching Saturn (7); they are Mars (3) in the same House, Uranus (0) is sextile and Rahu (8) at right angle.

His mother's death
The birth chart of Prince William

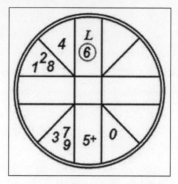

Thai astrology date: Monday
Calendar Tuesday 22 June 1982 at 03.03

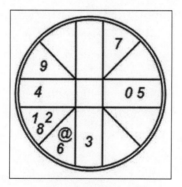

Chart of planets in transit
on 31 August 1997
Thai astrology date: 1 September 1997

The death of his mother occurs when he is 15. Between the ages of 15 and 17, the first (Self) House in transit, @, is in Virgo.

The first risk is indicated in the birth chart. In Virgo, there are two Maleficent planets, Mars (3) and Saturn (7). Therefore while @ is in Virgo, he faces the risk of opposition, difficulties or sorrow.

More indications can be seen in the chart of planets in transit as follows:

(A) In relation to @ in Virgo, the fourth (Home) House related to mother is Sagittarius. Its Ruler, Jupiter (5), in transit is in Capricorn. It is in Fall position, therefore, the planet representing mother is especially weak.

(B) Jupiter (5) in transit, representing mother, is in conjunction with Uranus (0) in transit. Uranus (0) is Co-Ruler of Aquarius, which is the sixth (Enemy) House from @.

(C) In Leo there is the Sun (1) which is the Ruler of Leo in its own House, therefore, strong. Leo is the twelfth House of sudden loss from @ in Virgo. The Sun (1), representing sudden loss, is in trine to Sagittarius, the House of mother.

(D) In Leo there is also Rahu (8) which is the Co-Ruler of Aquarius. Aquarius is the sixth (Enemy) House from @ in Virgo. Rahu (8), representing enemy, is also in trine to the House of mother. This is the final indication.

His father's reign

The day that we see Prince Charles ascending to the throne can also be linked to Prince William's chart below:

The birth chart of Prince William

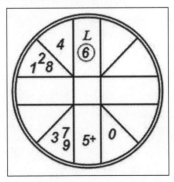

Thai astrology date: Monday
Calendar Tuesday 22 June 1982 at 03.03

189

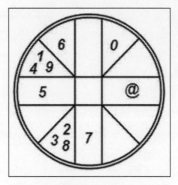

**Chart of planets in transit
on 5 July 2014**

The period that we see Prince Charles ascending to the throne is when Prince William's age is 33. Between the ages of 32 and 36, his first (Self) House in transit, @, is in Capricorn.

For a man, the Houses that are related to father are both the ninth (Exaltation) House and the tenth (Career) House. Here the indication is clearer in the tenth (Career) House in transit. In relation to @ in Capricorn, the tenth (Career) House is Libra. Therefore, while @ is in Capricorn, Libra represents father.

In the birth chart, there is Jupiter (5) in Libra. If we start from Libra as the first (Self) House of his father, as if his father's Lagna is in Libra, then having Jupiter (5) in conjunction with Lagna is the Special Position for Success of people with Lagna in Libra, a Human sign. This is the first indication of success to his father.

In the birth chart, Jupiter (5) has three planets in trine in Gemini, the Sun (1) its Friendly Pair, the Moon (2) its Element Pair and Rahu (8) the Ruler of Aquarius, the eleventh (Luck) from Lagna. All three planets therefore strengthen Jupiter (5).

In the transit chart, Saturn (7) is in Libra, now the House that represents father. Saturn (7) is the Ruler of @, also representing self in transit. Saturn (7) is in Exalted position. This indicates high honor to occur to both his father and himself.

Again, we can repeat the step in the birth chart by starting from Libra in the transit chart as the first (Self) House of his father, as if his father's Lagna in transit is in Libra. Then Saturn (7), which is in Exalted position, is in conjunction with his father's Lagna, also the Special Position for Success for people with Lagna in Libra, a Human sign. This indicates the strong possibility of his father's success.

We continue to use Libra as his father's Lagna in transit, and then the tenth (Career) House is Cancer. In the transit chart, there is Jupiter (5) in Cancer. It is in Exalted position. An especially strong Beneficent planet is in transit in the House that represents his father's career, another indication.

In relation to his father's Lagna in transit in Libra, the ninth (Exaltation) House is Gemini. There are two auspicious planets in transit in Gemini. Mercury (4) is strong in Ruler position. Ketu (9), the planet of royalty, is also strong in Gemini. They all add their strength to the House of exaltation of his father.

Mercury (4) is especially auspicious because it is also the Ruler of Virgo. In relation to @ in Capricorn, Virgo is the ninth (Exaltation) House. Mercury (4) in transit, therefore, represents his own honor. It transits into the House of his father's honor.

These two strong planets are also in trine with Libra, the House that represents his father, in our opinion confirming his father's ascension.

Love

His marriage may be late. This is indicated by Venus (6). Venus (6) is the Ruler of Libra, which is the seventh (Spouse) House from Tanu-kaset. Venus (6), representing spouse, is in Insecure position. This indicates a risk of a long and frustrating selection process, or the risk of failure to early romances.

In the seventh (Spouse) House there is also Jupiter (5). Jupiter (5) is the planet of elders. It indicates that the elders can be exerting strong influence or guidance over matters related to his spouse. Fortunately, Venus (6) itself is Tanu-kaset, and therefore will recover over time and result in a happy marriage, despite the long selection process.

In relation to Tanu-kaset (Venus (6) in Aries), the ninth (Exaltation) House is Sagittarius. Its Ruler is Jupiter (5) which is in Libra, the seventh (Spouse) House from Lagna. This indicates an elevation in status, honor after marriage.

His marriage
The birth chart of Prince William

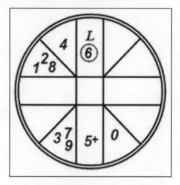

Thai astrology date: Monday
Calendar Tuesday 22 June 1982 at 03.03

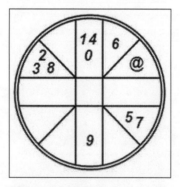

Chart of planets in transit
on 9 May 2019

This book is written in 2009. Based on the planet positions that can be calculated in advance, we believe that if the birth time is correct he will marry in 2019.

The most likely period for his marriage is between the ages of 37 to 39, when his first (Self) House in transit, @, is in Aquarius.

The first indication is shown in the birth chart. In relation to @ in Aquarius, the seventh (Spouse) House is Leo. The Ruler of Leo is the Sun (1). Therefore, while @ is in Aquarius, the Sun (1) represents spouse.

In the birth chart, the Sun (1) is in Gemini. In relation to @ in Aquarius, Gemini is the fifth House of youth, sudden luck. Therefore, while @ is in Aquarius, Gemini represents sudden luck.

The planet that now represents spouse in the House that now represents sudden luck is the first indication.

In the birth chart, Leo, now the House that represents spouse, is in sextile with Jupiter (5). Jupiter (5) is the Ruler of Sagittarius. In relation to @ in Aquarius, Sagittarius is the eleventh (Luck) House. Therefore, while @ is in Aquarius, Jupiter (5) also represents luck.

The planet that now represents luck in the position to reach the House that now represents spouse is the second indication.

In the birth chart, Jupiter (5) is also in trine with the Sun (1) and can influence each other. While @ is in Aquarius, the Sun (1) represents spouse, and Jupiter (5) represents luck. Luck is able to reach spouse while @ is in Aquarius.

In the transit chart, the Sun (1) which represents spouse is in Aries, in conjunction with Lagna. The Sun (1) is in Exalted position, especially strong. The planet that now represents spouse reaches self, Lagna in the birth chart.

In the transit chart, Jupiter (5), which represents luck, is in Sagittarius. It is strong in Ruler position. Jupiter (5) that now represents luck is in trine with the Sun (1) that now represents spouse is another indication. Jupiter (5) in transit is also in trine with Lagna in Aries. This is the third indication in the transit chart.

We, therefore, see his marriage occurring between the 14 April and 15 May 2019.

Barrack Obama

We believe this to be the birth chart of Barrack Obama, President of the United States of America in 2009, at the time of writing of this book. He was born on Friday 4 August 1961 at 19.24 in Honolulu, Hawaii, USA, GMT-10.00. His parents were separated in 1963. He was married in 1992 and had children in 1998 and 2001. He was elected Senator in 1996, 1998 and 2002 and President in 2008.

We have not obtained official verification of the birth time, therefore, cannot claim without any doubt that it is his birth chart.

The birth chart of Barrack Obama

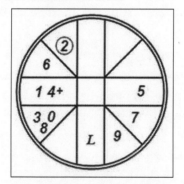

Thai astrology date: Saturday
Calendar Saturday 5 August 1961 at 12.24
Sunrise at 06.03

Self

Mercury (4) is Tanu-set and it is in Cancer. Cancer has the Moon (2) as its Ruler. The Moon (2) and Mercury (4) are the Friendly Pair; therefore, Mercury (4) is strong in this zodiac sign.

194

Mercury (4) is the planet of intelligence, speech and writing. With strong Mercury (4), he is a persuasive speaker, able to move the masses, and succeed in the task that requires clear explanation and piercing verbal flare.

Mercury (4) is also in the same sign with the Sun (1). This pair indicates the man of knowledge. Normally Mercury (4) is blinded by the Sun (1) when it is within 3 degrees of each other as happens in this case. However, Mercury (4) during his birth is unusually fast; hence, its good quality is not affected.

The Moon (2) is Tanu-kaset. It is also the Ruler of Cancer, the tenth (Career) House; therefore, it represents career. It is in Exalted position in Taurus. It indicates an especially important and famous career.

However, The Moon (2) in Taurus is in the eighth (Death) House from Lagna, and this is the Special Position of Hardship. He will feel heavy burden, face a lot of difficulties. He also views his own achievement as somewhat inadequate.

The Moon (2), Tanu-kaset, in the House that is related to death and separation indicates that he resettles abroad far away from his birth place.

In relation to Tanu-kaset, the third (Friend) House is Cancer. The Moon (2) is the Ruler of Cancer which represents siblings and close friends. The planet that represents friend in the House of death indicates that he lives far away from them.

The Moon (2), Tanu-kaset, has Ketu (9), the planet of high honor, directly opposite, enabling him to make exceptional achievement.

In relation to Lagna, the Ruler of the first (Self) House is Venus (6). It is in Gemini, which is the ninth (Exaltation) House from Lagna. The planet that represents self in the House of exaltation indicates a man preoccupied with the achievement of honor.

However, Venus (6) has its Enemy Pair, Saturn (7), directly opposite. It indicates that his strive for honor is opposed, or costly.

Work

In relation to Tanu-kaset in Taurus, the ninth (Exaltation) House is Capricorn. The Ruler of Capricorn is Saturn (7); therefore, Saturn (7) represents exaltation. It is in Sagittarius. Sagittarius is the third (Friend) House from Lagna. Saturn (7) in the third House from Lagna is the Special Position of Plenty for people with Lagna in Libra.

The planet that represents exaltation in the Special Position indicates exceptional success in his work. However, Saturn (7) is also the planet of heavy burden.

In relation to Tanu-kaset (the Moon (2) in Taurus), the eleventh (Luck) House is Pisces. The Ruler of Pisces is Jupiter (5); therefore, Jupiter (5) represents luck.

Jupiter (5) is in Capricorn, the fourth (Home) House from Lagna. This is his most important planet because it is in both the Special Position of Lotus and the Special Position of Plenty, making it exceptionally strong. The planet that represents luck in double Special Positions indicates exceptional career success.

Jupiter (5) also swaps Ruler positions with Saturn (7), making both Pseudo Rulers. It means that his success takes a long time but will continue to the end of life.

Jupiter (5) is also strengthened by the Sun (1), its Friendly Pair, and Mercury (4), a Beneficent planet, in the opposite House. The Sun (1) is in Perseverance position, active and working overtime, while Mercury (4) is the planet of diplomacy. They indicate that the problems can be tackled through the use of knowledge and diplomacy.

In relation to Tanu-kaset (the Moon (2) in Taurus), the tenth (Career) House is Aquarius. The Co-Rulers of Aquarius are Rahu (8) and Uranus (0) which are both in Leo. Leo is the eleventh (Luck) House from Lagna. Both planets that represent career in the House of luck indicate a very successful career.

In the tenth (Career) House from Lagna there are the Sun (1) and Mercury (4). The Sun (1) is the Ruler of the eleventh (Luck)

House from Lagna, and Mercury (4) is the Ruler of the ninth (Exaltation) House from Lagna. The planet that represents luck and another that represents honor in the House of career reconfirms exceptional career success.

Love

In relation to Tanu-kaset in Taurus, the seventh (Spouse) House is Scorpio. The Ruler of Scorpio is Mars (3); therefore, Mars (3) represents spouse. Mars (3) is in Leo, the House of luck from Lagna.

The planet that represents spouse in the House of luck indicates that he enjoys strong support from his spouse. The active nature of Mars (3) suggests that she is decisive, action oriented. Venus (6), the planet of love, has Saturn (7), its Enemy Pair, directly opposite, but is not affected because Saturn (7) is in the Special Position.

In relation to Tanu-kaset in Taurus, the second (Income) House is Gemini and the fifth (Children) House is Virgo. Both Gemini and Virgo have Mercury (4) as their Ruler. Mercury (4), therefore, represents income and youth. Mercury (4) is in Cancer, and Cancer is the tenth (Career) House from Lagna. The planet that represents income and youth in the House of career indicates that his income is from work that is supported by younger people.

His first presidential election
The birth chart of Barrack Obama

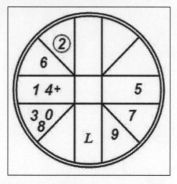

Thai astrology date: Saturday
Calendar Saturday 5 August 1961 at 12.24

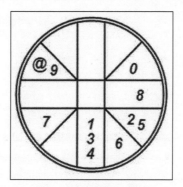

Chart of planets in transit
on 3 November 2008

It occurs at the age of 48. Between the ages of 48 and 52, the first (Self) House in transit, @, is in Gemini.

In the birth chart, Gemini has Saturn (7) in the opposite House. Saturn (7) is in the Special Position. A strong Saturn (7) opposite @ is the first indication.

In the birth chart, Leo is the third (Friend) House from @ in Gemini. Rahu (8) and Uranus (0) are in Leo. In relation to @ in Gemini, the ninth (Exaltation) House is Aquarius. The Co-Rulers of Aquarius are Rahu (8) and Uranus (0). Therefore, while @ is in Gemini, both Rahu (8) and Uranus (0) represent honor. The planets in the birth chart that now represent honor in the House of friend indicate strong support from friends and colleagues.

In the birth chart, Rahu (8) is particularly strong because it is in trine with Saturn (7) in Sagittarius. Saturn (7) is its Friendly Pair, and this is the pair of 'big' planets. Therefore, when they reach each other, they give big results to the person, either good or bad. While @ is in Gemini, Rahu (8) represents exaltation. The quality that Rahu (8) exerts on Saturn (7) is good.

In the birth chart, in Leo there is also Mars (3). Mars (3) is the Ruler of Aries. In relation to @ in Gemini, Aries is the eleventh (Luck) House. Therefore, while @ is in Gemini, Mars (3) represents luck. The planet in the birth chart that now represents luck is in conjunction with the planet that now represents exaltation.

However, Mars (3) is also the Ruler of Scorpio, the sixth (Enemy) House, indicating that success must be earned through a struggle. In Scorpio there is Ketu (9), the planet of advanced age and seniority, indicating an older opponent.

While @ is in Gemini, the Houses that are important to his career are Aquarius, the ninth (Exaltation) House, and Pisces, the tenth (Career) House. Their Rulers are Uranus (0) and Jupiter (5). In the transit chart, Uranus (0) is strong in Aquarius in Ruler position. Jupiter (5) is especially strong in Sagittarius in Ruler position. It is in conjunction with the Moon (2) in transit, its Element Pair, making it stronger. Jupiter (5) in transit in the third House from Lagna is also the Special Position of Plenty, another strong indication.

In the birth chart, in relation to Tanu-kaset (the Moon (2) in Taurus), the ninth (Exaltation) House is Capricorn. The Ruler of Capricorn is Saturn (7). Therefore, Saturn (7) represents exaltation.

In the transit chart, Saturn (7) is in Leo, which is the eleventh (Luck) House from Lagna. The planet that represents exaltation is in the House of luck. Saturn (7) in the eleventh House from Lagna is also the Special Position of Plenty for people with Lagna in Libra, a Human sign, adding to the chance.

The Ruler of the first (Self) House in transit, @, is Mercury (4). In the transit chart, Mercury (4) is in Libra, in conjunction with Lagna. Self in transit reaches self in the birth chart, strengthening self. Mercury (4) in conjunction with Lagna is also the Special Position for Success for people with Lagna in Libra, a Human sign. This makes Mercury (4) in transit especially strong.

In relation to @ in Gemini, the ninth (Exaltation) House is Aquarius. Rahu (8) is a Co-Ruler of Aquarius. Therefore, while @ is in Gemini, Rahu (8) represents exaltation. In the transit chart, Rahu (8) is in Capricorn. Rahu (8) in the fourth House from Lagna is an adverse position. It brings concern and a heavy heart. Ranu (8) is also strong in its Perseverance position, making his job especially difficult and challenging. He took office during one of the biggest financial crises in history.

His second presidential election
The birth chart of Barrack Obama

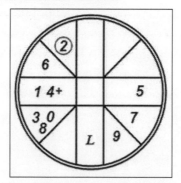

Thai astrology date: Saturday
Calendar Saturday 5 August 1961 at 12.24

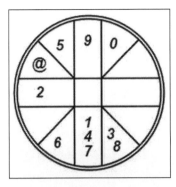

**Chart of planets in transit
on 6 November 2012**

This book is written in 2009. Based on the planet positions that can be calculated in advance, we believe that if the birth time is correct he will be re-elected in 2012.

His re-election occurs on 6 November 2012 at the age of 52. Between the ages of 48 and 52, the first (Self) House in transit, @, is still in Gemini.

In relation to @ in Gemini, the ninth (Exaltation) House is Aquarius. Saturn (7) and Rahu (8) are Co-Rulers of Aquarius; therefore, while @ is in Gemini, both planets represent exaltation.

In the transit chart, Saturn (7) is in Libra. It is in conjunction with Lagna and also especially strong in Exalted position. The planet that represents honor reaches self. Saturn (7) in transit in the same House as Lagna is also the Special Position for Success for people with Lagna in Libra, a Human sign.

In the transit chart, Rahu (8) is also strong in Exalted position in Scorpio. Rahu (8) in transit is also in conjunction with Mars (3) in transit, its Element Pair, making it stronger. While Rahu (8) is in the second (Income) House from Lagna, it also acts as the Leading engine for Lagna; hence, it can exert more influence on Lagna than when it is in other Houses. Rahu (8) is another planet that represents exaltation.

Mars (3), which is in conjunction with Rahu (8), is especially auspicious. Mars (3) is the Ruler of Aries. In relation to @ in Gemini, Aries is the eleventh (Luck) House. Therefore, while @ is in Gemini, Mars (3) represents luck. The planet that represents luck reaches the planet that represents exaltation.

In the transit chart, both the Sun (1) and Mercury (4) are in Libra, in conjunction with Lagna. The Sun (1) is in the Special Position for Success, and Mercury (4) is in the Special Position of Plenty, for people with Lagna in Libra, a Human sign.

We, therefore, see him winning the second presidential election in 2012.

George W Bush

We believe this to be the birth chart of George W Bush, born on Saturday 6 July 1946 at 07.26 in New Haven, Connecticut, USA, GMT-05.00. He was married on 5 November 1977 and had children in 1981. He was elected state governor in 1994 and 1998, and President in 2000 and 2004.

We have not obtained official verification of the birth time therefore cannot claim without any doubt that this is his birth chart.

The birth chart of George W Bush

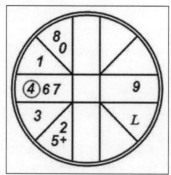

Thai astrology date: Saturday
Calendar Saturday 6 July 1946 at 19.26
Sunrise at 05.55

His Lagna is in Sagittarius, indicating a man of action, ready to volunteer, with a love of challenging and daring situations, impatient.

Jupiter (5) is Tanu-set in Virgo. It indicates a man of knowledge and always wanting to show it. He holds on to strict principles; a man who sets policy and strategies.

Mercury (4) is Tanu-kaset in Cancer. Mercury (4) is in conjunction with Venus (6), its Element Pair, and therefore especially strong. This is the water Element Pair in Cancer, the Cardinal water sign, therefore, the pair is in its strongest place. They give him strong determination, decisive actions, seriousness, and a strong unwavering goal.

In relation to Tanu-kaset (Mercury (4) in Cancer), Venus (6) is the Ruler of Libra, the fourth (Home) House, and of Taurus, the eleventh (Luck) House. Venus (6) is strong in Assistance position. The planet that represents family (Home) and luck reaches self, Mercury (4), Tanu-kaset. It indicates strong support both from his parents and from his colleagues.

For a man, the House that represents father is both the ninth (Exaltation) House and the tenth (Career) House. In the birth chart, the best indication about his father is the tenth (Career) House from Tanu-kaset (Mercury (4) in Cancer), which is Aries. The Ruler of Aries is Mars (3).

Mars (3), the planet that represents his father, is in Leo, which is the ninth (Exaltation) House from Lagna. The planet that represents father in the House of honor indicates a father of the ruling class, high position and honor.

What indicates that his father is also a President?

We can read the matters about his father as if Aries is the first House of his father's birth chart. The House that indicates his father's career is the tenth (Career) House from Aries. It is Capricorn. There is Ketu (9), the planet of high honor and royalty, in Capricorn. This is the first indication.

Mars (3) the planet that represents his father is in sextile with

203

the Sun (1) in Gemini. The Sun (1) is the Ruler of Leo which is the ninth (Exaltation) House from Lagna. The Sun (1), therefore, represents honor. The planet that represents honor reaching the planet that represents father is the second indication. The Sun (1) is also strong in Assistance position, making its enhancement to Mars (3) more powerful.

Capricorn, the House that represents the career of his father, is arrow clamped by many auspicious planets. There are the Sun (1), Mars (3), as well as the Element Pair of Mercury (4) and Venus (6), as well as Saturn (7), the Ruler of the seventh (Spouse) House from Tanu-kaset. All indicate an exceptionally high position for his father.

These planets also indicate an exceptionally high position for him. His Tanu-kaset, Mercury (4), is also clamped by these auspicious planets, with Venus (6) and Saturn (7) in conjunction, the Sun (1) on one side, Mars (3) on the other side, and Ketu (9) opposite.

Another pair that ensures his own success is the Moon (2) and Jupiter (5), the Element Pair, in Virgo. This is the earth Element Pair, and Virgo is the zodiac sign of earth element. They are in the tenth (Career) House from Lagna, making for a strong and famous career.

His work is not easy. Jupiter (5) is the Ruler of Sagittarius, which is the sixth (Enemy) House from Tanu-kaset, Mercury (4) in Cancer. This indicates opposition, frustration and challenges to his career. Fortunately, Jupiter (5) is in Insecure position, lessening the adverse affect. The problems can be solved over time.

Jupiter (5) is also the Ruler of Pisces, which is the ninth (Exaltation) House from Tanu-kaset (Mercury (4) in Cancer). The planet that represents honor in the House of career together with its Element Pair indicates a famous and honorable career.

His first presidential election
The birth chart of George W Bush

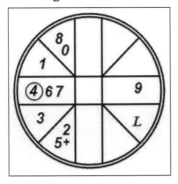

Thai astrology date: Saturday
Calendar Saturday 6 July 1946 at 19.26

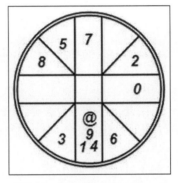

Chart of planets in transit
on 7 November 2000

The 7 November 2000 presidential election occurs at the age of 55. Between the ages of 54 and 58, the first (Self) House in transit, @, is in Libra.

In the birth chart, in relation to @ in Libra, the eleventh (Luck) House is Leo. The Ruler of Leo is the Sun (1). Therefore, while @ is in Libra, the Sun (1) represents luck. The Sun (1) is also strong in Assistance position.

In the birth chart, the Sun (1) is in Gemini, and Gemini is the ninth (Exaltation) House from @ in Libra. The planet that now represents luck in the House that now represents honor is the first indication.

In the birth chart, in relation to @ in Libra, the tenth (Career) House is Cancer. Therefore, while @ is in Libra, Cancer is the House that represents career. And Gemini is the House that represents honor. The Ruler of Gemini is Mercury (4). In the birth chart, Mercury (4) is in Cancer. The planet that represents honor is in the House that now represents career.

In the birth chart, the Sun (1) is in Gemini. In relation to @ in Libra, Gemini is the ninth (Exaltation) House. Therefore, while @ is in Libra, the Sun (1) represents honor. In the transit chart, the Sun (1) is in conjunction with @ in Libra. The planet that represents honor is in the House that now represents self. For @ in Libra, a Human sign, the Sun in conjunction with @ is also the Special Position for Success.

The Sun (1) is the Ruler of Leo. In relation to @ in Libra, Leo is the eleventh (Luck) House. Therefore, while @ is in Libra, the Sun (1) also represents luck. In the transit chart, the Sun (1) is in Libra, and in the birth chart Libra is the eleventh (Luck) House from Lagna. The planet that represents luck in the House of luck is another strong indication.

In relation to @ in Libra, Mercury (4) is the Ruler of Gemini which is the ninth (Exaltation) House from @ in Libra. Therefore, while @ is in Libra, Mercury (4) also represents honor. In the transit chart, Mercury (4) is in conjunction with @ in Libra. Honor reaches self. Mercury (4) in conjunction with @ in Libra, a Human sign, is also in the Special Position for Success.

In the transit chart, Mercury (4) in Libra is the eleventh (Luck) House from Lagna. The planet that represents honor is in the House of luck.

Finally, in the transit chart, there is Ketu (9), the planet of high honor and royalty, in conjunction with @ in Libra.

His second presidential election
The birth chart of George W Bush

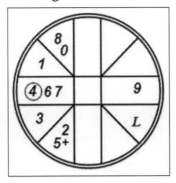

Thai astrology date: Saturday
Calendar Saturday 6 July 1946 at 19.26

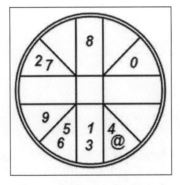

Chart of planets in transit
on 2 November 2004

The 2 November 2004 presidential election occurs at the age of 59. Between the ages of 59 and 68, the first (Self) House in transit, @, is in Scorpio.

In the birth chart, in relation to @ in Scorpio, the ninth (Exaltation) House is Cancer. Therefore, while @ is in Scorpio, Cancer is the House that represents honor. Mercury (4) and Venus (6), the especially strong water Element Pair, are in this House which represents honor. This is the first indication.

The Ruler of Cancer is the Moon (2). Therefore, while @ is in Scorpio, the Moon (2) represents honor. In the birth chart, the Moon (2) is in Virgo. The Moon (2) is especially strong in Assistance position, and is together with Jupiter (5), its earth Element Pair in the zodiac sign of earth element. In relation to @ in Scorpio, Virgo is also the eleventh (Luck) House. The planet that represents honor is in the House that represents luck.

In the birth chart, Saturn (7) is in Cancer. In relation to @ in Scorpio, Cancer is the ninth (Exaltation) House. Therefore, while @ is in Scorpio, Saturn (7) represents honor. In the transit chart, there is Saturn (7) in Gemini. It is opposite to Lagna in the birth chart. The planet that represents honor can reach self, Lagna. Saturn (7) in the eight House from Lagna in Sagittarius, a Human sign, is also the Special Position of Plenty.

In the birth chart, Mercury (4) is in Cancer, and therefore also represents honor. In the transit chart, Mercury (4) is in conjunction with @ in Scorpio. The planet that represents honor reaches self.

Gordon Brown

We believe this to be the birth chart of Gordon Brown, Prime Minister of United Kingdom in 2009, at the time of writing of this book. He was born on Tuesday 20 February 1951 in Scotland, GMT+00.00. He was married on 3 August 2000 and had 3 children in 2002, 2003 and 2006, the first child passed away soon after birth. He was Chancellor in 1997 and Prime Minister in 2007.

We construct the birth chart based on his past events. We place his Lagna in Leo, estimating the birth time to be between 16.39 and 19.01 Thai time, equal to between 09.39 and 12.01 at GMT+00.00. We, therefore, cannot claim without any doubt that this is his birth chart.

The birth chart of Gordon Brown

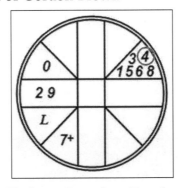

Thai astrology date: Tuesday
Calendar Tuesday 20 February 1951, 16.39-19.01
Sunrise at 06.39

Lagna in Leo indicates someone who is proud, wants to be a leader, and is ready to look after his people, his followers.

Tanu-set is Saturn (7) in Virgo. Saturn (7) as Tanu-set indicates a person that is pensive, serious, formal, and conservative, too much worry and too much repetitive thought.

In relation to Lagna, the Ruler of the first (Self) House is the Sun (1). It is in the seventh (Spouse) House. There are as many as six planets in the seventh (Spouse) House, indicating too much thought process in spouse selection. The Sun (1) being in Insecure position also makes initial success uncertain and the process quite long.

Frustration to his early romance is indicated by having Mars (3), Venus (6) and Rahu (8) in the seventh (Spouse) House from Lagna; all are Special Positions of Hardship.

On the other hand, Mercury (4), Tanu-kaset, being in conjunction with as many as six planets makes him successful. Many of these planets are in Special positions, making him highly successful in his career and eventually wealthy.

In relation to Tanu-kaset (Mercury (4) in Aquarius), the ninth (Exaltation) House is Libra. The Ruler of Libra is Venus (6).

Venus (6) in Aquarius is in conjunction with Tanu-kaset, the Result in High Exaltation. This indicates high honor in his career.

In relation to Tanu-kaset (Mercury (4) in Aquarius), the second (Income) House is Pisces and the eleventh (Luck) House is Sagittarius. Jupiter (5) is the Ruler of both signs, and it is in conjunction with Tanu-kaset, the Result in High Luck. This indicates substantial earnings. By Taksa, Jupiter (5) represents Success. The planet of success in conjunction with Tanu-kaset indicates a man of high principles, high moral standard and the ability to generate income.

The Sun (1) together with Mercury (4) is the knowledge pair. This pair is in conjunction with Tanu-kaset, indicating a man of intelligence, capability, and fine leadership.

In relation to Tanu-kaset (Mercury (4) in Aquarius), the fourth (Home) House that represents mother is Taurus. Its Ruler is Venus (6). The tenth (Career) House that represents father is Scorpio. Its Ruler is Mars (3). Both Mars (3) and Venus (6) are in Aquarius, the seventh (Spouse) House from Lagna. Both are the Special Positions of Hardship, indicating weak support from his parents. He builds his own life.

Rahu (8) is the planet of power. It is in Aquarius, strong in Ruler position. It is in conjunction with Tanu-kaset, indicating the love of politics.

Uranus (0), the planet of sudden loss, is in Gemini, the fifth (Children) House from Tanu-kaset. This perhaps explains the risk of one of his children passing away soon after birth.

His appointment as Prime Minister
The birth chart of Gordon Brown

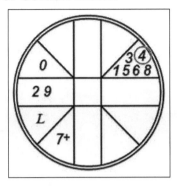

Thai astrology date: Tuesday
Calendar Tuesday 20 February 1951,
16.39-19.01

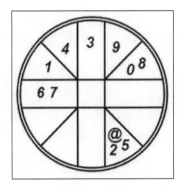

Chart of planets in transit
on 27 June 2007

It occurs at the age of 57. During the ages of 53 and 60, the first (Self) House in transit, @, is in Scorpio.

In the birth chart, in relation to @ in Scorpio, the ninth (Exaltation) House is Cancer. In Cancer, there is the Moon (2) which is strong in Ruler position. There is also Ketu (9), the planet of high honor. This shows that while @ is in Scorpio, the House of honor (in relation to @) is very strong, the first indication of a major career advance.

In relation to @ in Scorpio, Jupiter (5) is in the fourth House. Jupiter (5) in the fourth House from @ is the Special Position of Lotus, a strong indication of success.

In relation to @ in Scorpio, the ninth Exaltation House is Cancer. Although the Ruler of Cancer is the Moon (2), its transit is very rapid therefore for observation of planet in transit Saturn (7) is also used as the Ruler of Cancer. Therefore, while @ is in Scorpio, Saturn (7) also represents honor. In the birth chart, Saturn (7) is in Virgo, and Virgo is the eleventh (Luck) House from @ in Scorpio. Honor is in the House of luck.

In the transit chart, Saturn (7) is in Cancer. Saturn (7), representing honor, is in the House of honor, another indication.

In the transit chart, Jupiter (5), which is the planet of Special Position of Lotus while @ is in Scorpio, is in conjunction with @ in Scorpio, a really strong indication. Jupiter (5) in Scorpio is strong because it is together with the Moon (2), its Element Pair, and also in Perseverance position.

In the transit chart, Mars (3) is strong in Aries in Ruler position. In relation to Lagna, Aries is the ninth (Exaltation) House. In relation to @ in Scorpio, Mars (3) is the Ruler of the first (Self) House. The planet representing self is in the House of honor.

In the transit chart, Ketu (9), the planet of high honor, is in Pisces, in trine with @ in Scorpio. In the birth chart, Ketu (9) is in Cancer, which is the ninth (Exaltation) House from @ in Scorpio. Therefore, Ketu (9) represents honor and in transit it can reach self, @.

In the birth chart, the Moon (2) is in Cancer, the ninth (Exaltation) House from @ in Scorpio. In the transit chart, the Moon (2) is also in conjunction with @ in Scorpio. The planet representing honor reaches self.

The next election

It is easier to foresee a political change with fixed terms, but more difficult in a parliamentary system where election can occur any time. You may see some adverse indications, but they can be about other aspects of his career and not the position as such.

This book is written in 2009 and if the birth time that we estimate is correct, we do not see him winning the next election.

The birth chart of Gordon Brown

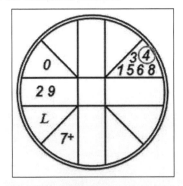

Thai astrology date: Tuesday
Calendar Tuesday 20 February 1951,
16.39-19.01

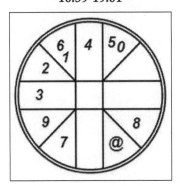

Chart of planets in transit on 17 May 2010

In May 2010, his age is 60. The first (Self) House in transit, @, is still in Scorpio.

While @ is in Scorpio, Rahu (8) is the Special Omen planet. In 2010 from his birthday in February, Rahu (8) represents Kali in transit. In the birth chart, Rahu (8) is strong in Ruler position and can reach Lagna. The planet that now becomes Kali in transit reaching self is the first indication of loss.

In relation to @ in Scorpio, Jupiter (5) is a very important planet because in the birth chart it is in the Special Position of Lotus. Unfortunately, in the transit chart, Jupiter (5) is now in the eighth (Death) House from Lagna, another bad indication. Jupiter (5) in transit is also opposite Saturn (7) in the birth chart, indicating lack of support from people in authority and the mass.

In relation to @ in Scorpio, Ruler of the first (Self) House is Mars (3). In the transit chart, Mars (3) is in the twelfth (Loss) House from Lagna. Self is in the House of loss.

In relation to @ in Scorpio, Ruler of the eighth (Death) House is Mercury (4). In the transit chart, Mercury (4) is in the ninth (Exaltation) House from Lagna. The planet representing death is in the House of honor.

It is unlikely that he will win the next election.

David Cameron

We believe this to be the birth chart of David Cameron, Leader of the Opposition in United Kingdom in 2009, at the time of writing of this book. He was born on Sunday 9 October 1966 in London, United Kingdom, GMT+00.00. He was married on 1 June 1996 and had 2 children in 2004 and 2006. He was Leader of the Opposition in 2005.

We construct the birth chart based on his profile and past events. We place his Lagna in Virgo, estimating the birth time to be between 04.08 and 06.56 Thai time, equal to between 21.08 and 23.56 at GMT+00.00. We, therefore, cannot claim without any doubt that this is his birth chart.

The birth chart of David Cameron

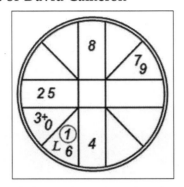

Thai astrology date: Sunday
Calendar Sunday 9 October 1966, 04.08-06.56
Sunrise at 06.08

Lagna in Virgo indicates a man of mild manner and soft appeal, who gets along with everybody; patient and intelligent.

Tanu-set is Mars (3) which indicates an autocratic person, able to make quick and decisive actions, who believes his own opinion.

Venus (6) is the Ruler of Libra, the second (Income) House. It is in conjunction with Lagna, indicating a man of wealth. Venus (6) in conjunction with Lagna is also the Special Position of Plenty for Lagna in Virgo, a Human sign, adding to wealth.

Tanu-kaset is the Sun (1) in Virgo. If his birth time is after 23.00 London time (after 06.00 in Thailand), the Thai astrology date is Sunday. This makes Mercury (4), the Ruler of the first (Self) House from Lagna, represent Success by way of Taksa. It indicates a strong family background.

Mercury (4) the Ruler of the first (Self) House from Lagna swaps Ruler positions with Venus (6) the Ruler of the second (Income) House from Lagna, indicating wealth.

In relation to Tanu-kaset (the Sun (1) in Virgo), Jupiter (5) is the Ruler of Sagittarius, the fourth (Home) House from Tanu-kaset, which represents his family background. Jupiter (5) in

Cancer is in the eleventh (Luck) House from Tanu-kaset. This indicates a very strong family background with real estates.

In relation to Tanu-kaset, the Moon (2) is the Ruler of the eleventh (luck) House. It is strong in Ruler position. It is also the planet of mother, indicating strong support from her.

In relation to Tanu-kaset, the seventh (Spouse) House is Pisces. Jupiter (5) is the Ruler of Pisces. It is in Cancer, strong in Exalted position and also in conjunction with the Moon (2), its Element Pair. This indicates a wealthy spouse of high society who is able to give him strong support.

In relation to Tanu-kaset, the ninth (Exaltation) House is Taurus. Venus (6) is the Ruler of Taurus. It is in conjunction with Lagna. This is the Result in High Exaltation, indicating high career success.

His election win
The birth chart of David Cameron

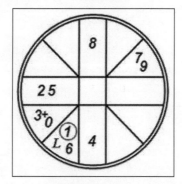

**Thai astrology date: Sunday
Calendar Sunday 9 October 1966,
04.08-06.56**

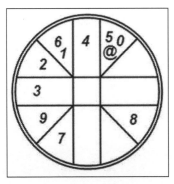

**Chart of planets in transit
on 17 May 2010**

May 2010 is when his age is 44. Between the ages of 38 and 44, the first (Self) House in transit, @, is in Pisces.

In relation to @, in Pisces, Jupiter (5) is the Ruler of the first (Self) House. In the birth chart, Jupiter (5) is especially strong in Exalted position in Cancer, the fifth (Children) House from @. This is the Special Position of Plenty for Lagna in Pisces, an Aquatic sign, the first indication of success.

In relation to @, in Pisces, Jupiter (5) is also the Ruler of the tenth (Career) House. In the transit chart, Jupiter (5) is strong in Ruler position in Pisces, in conjunction with @ and opposite to Lagna. The planet representing both career and sudden luck can reach both versions of self.

In relation to @, in Pisces, Saturn (7) is the Ruler of the eleventh (Luck) House. In the transit chart, it is in conjunction with Lagna. The planet representing luck has reached self. Saturn (7) together with Lagna is also the Special Position for Lagna in Virgo.

In relation to @, in Pisces, Mars (3) is also the Ruler of the ninth (Exaltation) House. In the transit chart, Mars (3) is in Cancer, the eleventh (Luck) House from Lagna. Mars (3) in the fifth House from @ is also the Special Position of Plenty.

This book is written in 2009. If the birth time that we estimated is correct, we see him becoming Prime Minister in May 2010.

Segolene Royal

We believe this to be the birth chart of Segolene Royal, a prominent French politician. She was born on Tuesday 22 September 1953 in Dakar, Senegal, GMT+00.00. She sued her father to force him to pay child support. She won a legislative election in 1988, and was first appointed minister in 1992. She lost the Presidential election in May 2007.

We construct the birth chart based on her past events. We place her Lagna in Aries, estimating the birth time to be between 20.24 and 22.23 Thai time, equal to between 13.24 and 15.23 at GMT+00.00. We, therefore, cannot claim without any doubt that this is her birth chart.

The birth chart of Segolene Royal

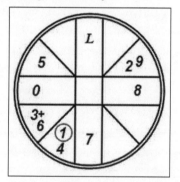

Thai astrology date: Tuesday
Calendar Tuesday 22 September 1953, 20.24 – 22.23
Sunrise at 06.07

Lagna in Aries indicates a woman of courage; bold, open, straightforward and dedicated; prepared to make sacrifices, expressive; shows her likes and dislikes clearly; she is a serious person.

Mars (3) is Tanu-set as well as the Ruler of the first (Self) House, shows an ambitious person who likes to win, serious in all matters no matter how trivial, serious in love and hate, does not forgive and forget easily; therefore, may appear a little strong and overpowering for a woman.

Mars (3), representing self, is in the fifth (Children) House, indicating a person who is very involved with her children, looking after them closely, very concerned about them.

The Sun (1) is Tanu-kaset in Virgo. It is in the sixth (Enemy) House from Lagna, indicating oppositions and competition in life. She has to struggle through youth, competing to win, and has the risk of building up personal debts early in life. However, the Sun (1) in the sixth (Enemy) House is the Special Position of Plenty, enabling her to win many of her fights.

Saturn (7) is in the seventh (Spouse) House from Lagna, the Special Position of Hardship. It causes difficulties with marriage. It also causes frequent changes of her living place.

In relation to Tanu-kaset (the Sun (1) in Virgo), the fifth (Children) House is Capricorn, whose Ruler is Saturn (7). Saturn (7) is also the Co-Ruler of Aquarius, the sixth (Enemy) House from Tanu-kaset. Therefore, Saturn (7) represents both children and enemy, and it is the planet of hardship.

Saturn (7) is opposite to Lagna. It indicates the burden caused by children, either in expenses or in maternal concern. Saturn (7) in Exalted position makes the problems more severe.

Mars (3) in the fifth (Children) House from Lagna is also the Special Position of Hardship, causing difficulty with her children. They can be difficult to control or difficult to be educated or be persuaded to follow her guidelines. By Taksa, Mars (3) also represents subordinates. Being the planet of hardship also indicates some difficulty with subordinates and close followers.

In relation to Tanu-kaset (the Sun (1) in Virgo), the fourth (Home) House that represents father is Sagittarius. Jupiter (5) is the Ruler of Sagittarius, and it is in Gemini. It is in Insecure position, indicating a father that is not well to do, or whose wealth can fluctuate through life.

In relation to Tanu-kaset, the sixth (Enemy) House is Aquarius, whose Ruler is Rahu (8). Rahu (8) is strong in Perseverance position in Capricorn, the tenth (Career) House from Lagna. It shows enemies related to her work. The enemies tend to be powerful, the character of Rahu (8).

In relation to Tanu-kaset, the ninth (Exaltation) House is Taurus, whose Ruler is Venus (6). Venus (6) is in Leo with Mars (3), its Friendly Pair, and indicating support from her colleagues.

In relation to Tanu-kaset, the tenth (Career) House is Gemini, whose Ruler is Mercury (4). Mercury (4) is in conjunction with Tanu-kaset, and is especially strong in Exalted position. The Sun (1) and Mercury (4) together with Tanu-kaset are the Result of High Leadership. This shows a person very capable of leadership, a good planner, a fine strategic thinker, one who attains a high administrative position an intelligent person.

In relation to Tanu-kaset, the eleventh (Luck) House is Cancer, whose Ruler is the Moon (2). The Moon (2) is in Aquarius, which is the eleventh (Luck) House from Lagna. This is the Result in High Luck, enabling the person to accumulate wealth over her lifetime and win the support of others, putting her in leadership positions.

The first presidential election
The birth chart of Segolene Royal

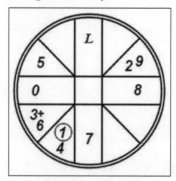

Thai astrology date: Tuesday
Calendar Tuesday 22 September 1953,
20.24 – 22.23

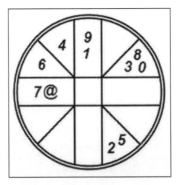

Chart of Planets in transit
on 5 May 2007

The first election occurs at the age of 54. Between the ages of 52 and 56, the first (Self) House in transit, @, is in Cancer.

In the birth chart, in relation to @ in Cancer, the ninth (Exaltation) House is Pisces. The Ruler of Pisces is Jupiter (5). Therefore, while @ is in Cancer, Jupiter (5) represents honor. In the birth chart, Jupiter (5) is in Gemini. Gemini is the twelfth (Loss) House from @ in Cancer. The planet that represents honor in the House that now represents loss gives disappointment.

The Moon (2), the planet of Special Position of Lotus in the birth chart in Aquarius is now in the eighth (Death) House in relation to @ in Cancer. It is now in a Special Position of Hardship in relation to @ in Cancer, the second indication.

In the transit chart, Jupiter (5) is in Scorpio, which is the eighth (Death) House from Lagna. This is the Special Position of Hardship for Lagna in Aries. The planet that represents honor is in hardship, and it is in the House of death.

221

The second presidential election
The birth chart of Segolene Royal

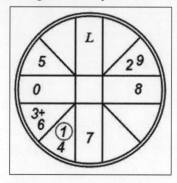

Thai astrology date: Tuesday
Calendar Tuesday 22 September 1953,
20.24 – 22.23

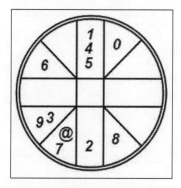

Chart of Planets in transit
on 5 May 2012

This book is written in 2009. If she runs again in 2012, it will be at the age of 59. Between the ages of 59 and 61, the first (Self) House in transit, @, is in Virgo.

In the birth chart, in relation to @ in Virgo, the ninth (Exaltation) House is Taurus, whose Ruler is Venus (6). Therefore, while @ is in Virgo, Venus (6) represents honor. In the birth chart, Venus (6) is in Leo. In relation to @ in Virgo, Leo is the twelfth

(Loss) House. The planet that represents honor in the House that now represents loss is not a good indication for success.

In fact, in relation to @ in Virgo, the Friendly Pair of Mars (3) and Venus (6) in Leo are now in the House of loss, there is a risk that her colleagues may even be reluctant to support her for this competition.

In relation to @ in Virgo, the tenth (Career) House is Gemini. In the birth chart, there is Jupiter (5) in Gemini; therefore, while @ is in Virgo, Jupiter (5) represents career. In the transit chart, Jupiter (5) is in Aries, the eighth (Death) House from @ in Virgo, indicating the possibility of another disappointment.

In relation to @ in Virgo, the sixth (Enemy) House is Aquarius whose Ruler is Rahu (8). In the transit chart, Rahu (8) is in Scorpio, opposite to Taurus, the ninth (Exaltation) House from @ in Virgo, indicating difficulty in matters related to honor.

Saturn (7), the Co-Ruler of Aquarius, also represents enemy. In the transit chart, Saturn (7) is in conjunction with @ in Virgo. The planet that represents enemy reaches self.

We see her chance of success in the 2012 election as very small.

Nicholas Sarkozy

We believe this to be the birth chart of Nicholas Sarkozy, President of France in 2009, at the time of writing of this book. He was born on Friday 28 January 1955 in Paris, France, GMT+01.00. He was first appointed minister in 1993. He was married in 1982, divorced in and remarried in 1996, and married the third time in 2008.

We construct the birth chart based on his past events. We place his Lagna in Cancer, estimating the birth time to be between 15.20 and 17.19 Thai time, equal to between 09.20 and 11.19 at GMT+01.00. We, therefore, cannot claim without any doubt that this is his birth chart.

The birth chart of Nicholas Sarkozy

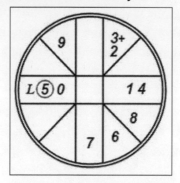

Thai astrology date: Friday
Calendar Friday 28 January 1955, 15.20 – 17.19
Sunrise at 06.00

Lagna in Cancer signifies a person who likes peace, an orderly life, and wants to take care of others.

The Moon (2), the Ruler of the first (Self) House is in the ninth (Exaltation) House from Lagna, indicating a strong pursuit of honor, high position, fame and respect.

Mars (3) as Tanu-set indicates a person with strong determination; he is hard working, ambitious, impatient, and short tempered; one that can hold on to his anger for some time.

Jupiter (5) is Tanu-kaset and is very strong in Exalted position. In relation to Tanu-kaset (Jupiter (5) in Cancer), it is also the Ruler of the ninth (Exaltation) House. This is the Result in High Exaltation, indicating a very high career position. The Moon (2), the Ruler of the first (Self) House from Tanu-kaset is in Pisces, which is the ninth (Exaltation) House from Lagna. The Moon (2) and Jupiter (5) are, therefore, in double exaltation positions, adding to his ability.

In relation to Tanu-kaset, the fourth (Home) House is Libra. There is Saturn (7) in Libra, especially strong in Exalted position, and is the Special Position of Plenty for people with Lagna in Cancer, an Aquatic sign. It indicates a well to do family of high society.

In relation to Tanu-kaset, the fifth (Children) House is Scorpio, and the tenth (Career) House is Aries. Mars (3) is the Ruler of both Houses. Mars (3) is in the ninth (Exaltation) House from Lagna, indicating a happy youth, with good education. It is also good for his work, with support from people all round.

In relation to Tanu-kaset, the fourth (Home) House is Libra, and the eleventh (Luck) House is Taurus. The Ruler of both Houses is Venus (6), which is in Scorpio, the fifth (Children) House from Lagna. The planet that represents family and luck is in the House of children and luck, confirming family support. Venus (6) in Insecure position would normally lessen the good quality. However, there is Saturn (7) in Exalted position in Libra, the House of which Venus (6) is the Ruler. The Insecure position of Venus (6) has, therefore, been recovered.

In relation to Tanu-kaset, the second (Income) House is Leo whose Ruler is the Sun (1). The Sun (1) is in the seventh (Spouse) House from Lagna, indicating that he receives good financial advice from his spouse; he builds up his wealth after marriage.

In relation to Tanu-kaset, the twelfth (Loss) House is Gemini whose Ruler is Mercury (4). Mercury (4) is in the seventh (Spouse) House from Lagna, indicating a risk to marriage. The Moon (2) is together with Mars (3), the troublesome pair, giving the tendency of many romantic affairs.

The first presidential election
The birth chart of Nicholas Sarkozy

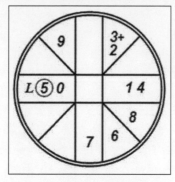

**Thai astrology date: Friday
Calendar Friday 28 January 1955,
20.24 – 22.23**

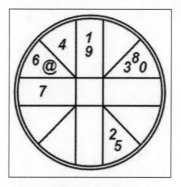

**Chart of Planets in transit
on 5 May 2007**

The first election occurs at the age of 53. Between the ages of 53 and 56, the first (Self) House in transit, @, is in Gemini.

In relation to @ in Gemini, the ninth (Exaltation) House is Aquarius whose Ruler is Rahu (8). Therefore, while @ is in Gemini, Rahu (8) represents honor. In the birth chart, Rahu (8) is in Sagittarius, opposite @ in Gemini. The planet that now represents honor reaches self.

Saturn (7) is a Co-Ruler of Aquarius, and therefore also represents honor while @ is in Gemini. In the birth chart, Saturn (7) is
in trine with Gemini, doubling the honor upon self, @, while in
Gemini.

In the transit chart, Rahu (8), the first planet of honor, is in
Aquarius. Even though it is the eighth (Death) House from
Lagna, Rahu (8) is still strong because it is in Ruler position.
Saturn (7), the second planet of honor, is in Cancer, in
conjunction with Lagna, bringing honor to self. This is especially
important because Saturn (7) is the planet of the mass, giving
him the support of the electorates.

Mars (3) represents career because in the birth chart it is in the
House of career in relation to @ in Gemini. Mars (3) in transit is
in the ninth (Exaltation) House from @. The planet that now
represents career is in the House of honor.

The second presidential election
The birth chart of Nicholas Sarkozy

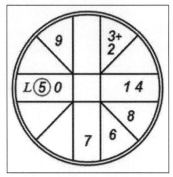

Thai astrology date: Friday
Calendar Friday 28 January 1955,
20.24 – 22.23

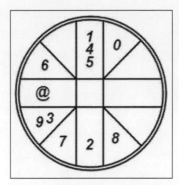

**Chart of Planets in transit
on 5 May 2012**

The next election is scheduled in 2012, at the age of 58. Between the ages of 57 and 62, the first (Self) House in transit, @, is in Cancer.

In relation to @ in Cancer, the ninth (Exaltation) House is Pisces whose Ruler is Jupiter (5). Therefore, while @ is in Cancer, Jupiter (5) represents honor. In the birth chart, Jupiter (5) is in conjunction with @, the clearest indication of another success.

In the transit chart, Jupiter (5) is in Aries. Aries is the tenth (Career) in relation to both @ and Lagna. The planet that now represents honor is in the House of career. Jupiter (5) in Aries is also strong in Assistance position.

This book is written in 2009. If the birth time that we estimated is correct, we see him winning again in May 2012.

Angela Merkel

We believe this to be the birth chart of Angela Merkel, the Chancellor of Germany in 2009, at the time of writing. She was born on Saturday 17 July 1954 at 17.45 in Hamburg, Germany, GMT+01.00. She was married in 1977 and divorced in 1982. She was first appointed cabinet minister in 1994, elected Chancellor in 2005.

We have not obtained official verification of the birth time;

therefore, cannot claim without any doubt that this is her birth chart.

The birth chart of Angela Merkel

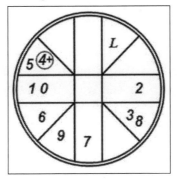

Thai astrology date: Sunday
Calendar Sunday 17 July 1954 at 23.45
Sunrise at 05.58

Lagna in Pisces indicates a plump person who enjoys food, loves justice, is kind hearted and soft hearted; she is a reasonable person who always deliberately weighs all options.

Mercury (4) as Tanu-set indicates a talkative person, an able communicator, a persuasive negotiator; she is untiring with her words which always seem reliable, dependable.

Jupiter (5) is the Ruler of the first (Self) House. It is in Gemini, the fourth (Home) House from Lagna, indicating her interest in building her family; a good mother who guides and watches her children closely.

Mercury (4) is both Tanu-set and Tanu-kaset, the Result in High Ability. It makes her a determined and highly able person with strong impetus to succeed.

In relation to Tanu-kaset (Mercury (4) in Gemini), the fourth (Home) House is Virgo, whose Ruler is also Mercury (4). Mercury in Gemini is in the fourth (Home) House from Lagna, indicating well to do parents with real estate holdings, as well as her own ability to build a strong home.

Jupiter (5) in the fourth (Home) House from Lagna is the Special Position of Lotus, giving her the ability to lead and hold high positions. The Moon (2), the Ruler of the second (Income) House from Tanu-kaset, is in Capricorn, the eleventh (Luck) from Lagna, indicating financial success.

In the seventh (Spouse) House from Tanu-kaset (Mercury (4) in Gemini), there are Mars (3) and Rahu (8), both in the Special Position of Hardship. They are also strong, being the wind Element Pair, indicating the risks to marriage.

In relation to Tanu-kaset, the ninth (Exaltation) House is Aquarius, whose Ruler is Rahu (8). Rahu (8) is in Sagittarius, the tenth (Career) House from Lagna. It indicates high career achievement.

In relation to Tanu-kaset, the eleventh (Luck) House is Aries, whose Ruler is Mars (3). Mars (3) is also in Sagittarius, the tenth (Career) House from Lagna. The planet of luck in the House of career reconfirms high achievement.

Appointment to Chancellor
The birth chart of Angela Merkel

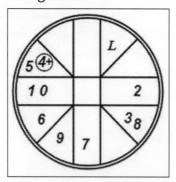

Thai astrology date: Sunday
Calendar Sunday 17 July 1954 at 23.45

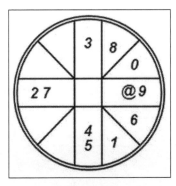

**Chart of Planets in transit
on 22 November 2005**

The appointment occurs at the age of 52. Between the ages of 47 and 52, the first (Self) House in transit, @, is in Capricorn.

In the birth chart, there is Saturn (7) in especially strong Exalted position in Libra. While @ is in Capricorn, Libra is the tenth House of career. Having an especially strong planet in the House of career is the first indication.

In the birth chart, there are also four Beneficent planets in clamp positions that can reach Capricorn. They are the Moon (2), Mercury (4), Jupiter (5) and Venus (6).

In the transit chart, Saturn (7), representing career, is in Cancer. In relation to Lagna, Cancer is the fifth (Children) House of sudden luck, and Saturn (7) is in the Special Position of Plenty.

The second term
The birth chart of Angela Merkel

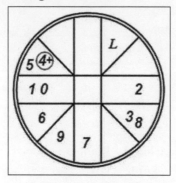

Thai astrology date: Sunday
Calendar Sunday 17 July 1954 at 23.45

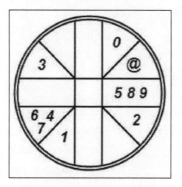

Chart of Planets in transit
on 27 September 2009

The next election is on 27 September 2009. We prepared the manuscript of this book in early 2009, but due to the long lead time for printing, the book may appear in the market after the result is already known.

We see her chance of reappointment to the second term in 2009 as very strong.

It occurs at her age of 56. Between the ages of 53 and 56, the first (Self) House in transit, @, is in Aquarius.

There are some very positive indications:

In the transit chart, there are three planets in Leo which are opposite to @. They are Mercury (4), Venus (6) and Saturn (7). All three are in the Special Position of Plenty in relation to @.

In the birth chart, in relation to @ in Aquarius, Mercury (4) in Gemini is in the fifth (Children) House which is related to sudden luck, Venus (6) is the Ruler of Libra, the ninth (Exaltation) House and Saturn (7) in Libra is in the ninth (Exaltation) House which are both related to honor. The planets in Special Positions in the transit chart are, therefore, all related to sudden luck and honor.

In the transit chart, Mars (3) in Gemini is the Special Position of Plenty for Lagna in Pisces. In relation to @ in Aquarius, Mars (3) is the Ruler of the tenth (Career) House. The planet related to career is, therefore, in the Special Position.

We, therefore, predict that she will win the second term as Chancellor.

Oprah Winfrey

We believe this to be the birth chart of Oprah Winfrey, born on Friday 29 January1954 at 04.30 in Kosciusko, Mississippi, USA, GMT-06.00. Early in life, she lived with her mother. She had a tragic premature birth in 1968. Her show business success started in 1984.

We have not obtained official verification of the birth time; therefore, cannot claim without any doubt that this is her birth chart.

The birth chart of Oprah Winfrey

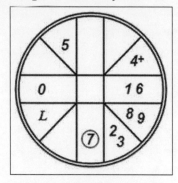

Thai astrology date: Friday
Calendar Friday 29 January 1954 at 17.30
Sunrise at 06.46

Her Lagna is in Leo indicating a woman of leadership; she is proud, and willing to look after other people, her team.

Her Tanu-set is Mercury (4) indicating a person of intelligence, with the gift of speech, communication, writing. Mercury (4) is in trine with, and enhanced by, Saturn (7), its Enhancement Pair. It gives her speeches more poise, more weight, and more things for listeners to think about.

Mercury (4) is Tanu-set in Aquarius. When Tanu-set is in Aquarius, the Ruler to be considered for Tanu-kaset is Saturn (7).

Saturn (7) is in Libra. It indicates a person of justice and righteousness. Saturn (7) is in Exalted position, indicating an enduring fighter, patient, strong, and willing to work through obstacles, eventually successful and famous.

By Taksa, Saturn (7) represents Toil, her work. It is also the Ruler of Aquarius. In relation to Tanu-kaset (Saturn (7) in Libra), Aquarius is the fifth (Children) House. Saturn (7), therefore, represents youth. This indicates work related to young people.

In relation to Lagna in Leo, Libra is the third (Friend) House, which is the House of communication. There is Saturn (7) in Libra. The planet that represents work and youth in the House of communication indicates work that appeals to a young audience.

By Taksa, Jupiter (5) represents elders. It is in Taurus, the tenth (Career) House from Lagna. It is in the Special Position for success for people with Lagna in Leo, a Quadruped sign. This indicates work about justice, righteousness, correcting the wrongs of society, and education which is the character of Jupiter (5). Its Special Position also makes her famous.

Jupiter (5) is the Ruler of Sagittarius and Pisces. In relation to Tanu-kaset (Saturn (7) in Libra), Sagittarius is the third (Friend) House representing communication and Pisces is the sixth (Enemy) House representing difficulties. It indicates work on issues of difficulties, social malice, and injustice.

In relation to Tanu-kaset, the second (Income) House is Scorpio. The Ruler of Scorpio is Mars (3). Mars (3) is in Scorpio and strong in Ruler position, indicating wealth. In relation to Lagna in Leo, Scorpio is the fourth (Home) House that is about real estate and property. This indicates a lot of wealth in the form of property.

Another strong indicator of wealth is shown by the Sun (1). It is the Ruler of Leo, the first (Self) House from Lagna, and therefore represents self. In relation to Tanu-kaset, Leo is the eleventh (Luck) House; therefore, the Sun (1) also represents luck. The Sun (1) is in Capricorn. In relation to Lagna in Leo, Capricorn is the sixth (Enemy) House. The Sun (1) in the sixth (Enemy) House is the Special Position of Plenty for people with Lagna in Leo, a Quadruped sign.

By Taksa, Venus (6) represents Followers, her helpers and her fans. Venus (6) is also the Ruler of Libra, the House that Saturn (7), Tanu-kaset, occupies. Venus (6) is in Capricorn, in conjunction with the Sun (1). Venus (6) in the sixth (Enemy) House is also the Special Position of Plenty. The planet that represents followers in the Special position indicates charm and young followers, a role model to young people.

Mercury (4) is the Ruler of Gemini. In relation to Tanu-kaset

(Saturn (7) in Libra), Gemini is the ninth (Exaltation) House. Therefore, Mercury (4) represents honor. Mercury (4) is in Aquarius, opposite to Lagna. The planet of speech that also represents honor can reach self, indicating success from communication.

However, Mercury (4) is also the Ruler of Virgo. In relation to Tanu-kaset (Saturn (7) in Libra), Virgo is the twelfth (Loss) House. Mercury (4) is in Aquarius which is in the seventh (Spouse) House from Lagna. The planet that represents loss in the House of spouse indicates risk from the opposite sex.

By Taksa, Rahu (8) represents Kali, the planet of difficulty and suffering. Rahu (8) is in Sagittarius. In relation to Lagna in Leo, Sagittarius is the fifth (Children) House. The planet of Kali in the House of youth indicates someone born and raised in difficult circumstances, a difficult early life. She has to fight her way through youth in adverse surroundings.

In relation to Tanu-kaset, the fifth (Children) House is Aquarius. The Co-Ruler of Aquarius is Uranus (0). Uranus (0) is in Cancer, which is the twelfth (Loss) House from Lagna. The planet that represents children in the House of loss indicates difficulties related to child birth, or pregnancy.

The risk to health is hinted by Jupiter (5) and Venus (6). Jupiter (5) is the Ruler of Pisces. In relation to Lagna in Leo, Pisces is the eighth (Death) House. Venus (6) is the Ruler of Taurus. In relation to Tanu-kaset (Saturn (7) in Libra), Taurus is the eighth (Death) House. They are in trine with each other. Both planets that represent illness can reach each other, which indicate health risks related to heart disease, diabetics.

Her Marriage?
The birth chart of Oprah Winfrey

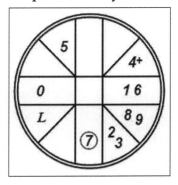

Thai astrology date: Friday
Calendar Friday 29 January 1954 at 17.30

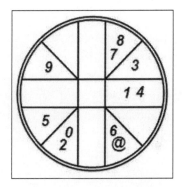

Chart of planet in transit
on 20 January 1968

This birth chart indicates someone who may fall in love at a tender age. Between the ages of 9 and 16, the first (Self) House in transit, @, is in Scorpio. In Scorpio, there is the Moon (2) and Mars (3), the troublesome pair of daring action mixed with romance. In Capricorn, there is also the Sun (1) and Venus (6), the pair that hints at an early marriage. These two planets are also in sextile with Scorpio, self in transit. The Moon (2) in Scorpio also has Jupiter (5) opposite. This is the pair of easy

237

romance. These are all strong setups for romantic affair while @ is in Scorpio.

There are also hints in the transit chart. In relation to @ in Scorpio, Jupiter (5) in the birth chart is in the seventh (Spouse) House. While @ is in Scorpio, therefore, Jupiter (5) represents spouse. In the transit chart, Jupiter (5) is in Leo. It is in conjunction with Lagna. The planet that represents spouse reaches self.

In relation to @ in Scorpio, Venus (6) is the Ruler of the seventh (Spouse) House. Venus (6), therefore, represents spouse. In the transit chart, Venus (6) is in Scorpio, in conjunction with @, self in transit. Again, the planet that represents spouse reaches self.

Her subsequent romance much later in life is more secure. In relation to Tanu-kaset (Saturn (7) in Libra), the seventh (Spouse) House is Aries. The Ruler of Aries is Mars (3). In the birth chart, Mars (3) in Scorpio is secure, the Ruler in its own House. This indicates a happy relationship that is warm and will last a lifetime. However, the chance of an official marriage may never occur because Mars (3) together with the Moon (2) emphasizes romance (substance) more than marriage (form).

Bill Gates III

We believe this to be the birth chart of Bill Gates III, born on Friday 28 October 1955 at 20.57 in Seattle, Washington, USA, GMT-08.00. He was married on 1 January 1994 and had children in 1996, 1999 and 2002. His initial business success started in 1980, with a major breakthrough in 1985.

We have not obtained official verification of the birth time, and therefore cannot claim without any doubt that this is his birth chart.

The birth chart of Bill Gates

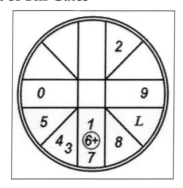

Thai astrology date: Saturday
Calendar Saturday 29 October 1955 at 11.57
Sunrise at 06.12

Lagna in Sagittarius indicates a person who likes challenges, daring situations, impatient and likes to volunteer.

Jupiter (5), the Ruler of the first (Self) House is in the ninth (Exaltation) House from Lagna, indicating a person who is preoccupied with progress in life, constantly seeking success and honor.

Venus (6) is Tanu-set, indicating a person who is artistic, imaginative, a dreamer who dwells on money and wealth.

Venus (6) is also Tanu-kaset, the Result in High Ability. The Sun (1) is in Fall position in Libra. But it is recovered by being in conjunction with Venus (6), Tanu-set.

This is the birth chart of a man with great wealth. What are the indications?

Venus (6) is in the eleventh (Luck) House from Lagna. This is the Special Position of Plenty for people with Lagna in Sagittarius, a Human sign. Venus (6) is strong in Ruler position. By Taksa, Venus (6) also represents Success, the second indication.

The second (Income) House from Lagna is Capricorn. Its Ruler is Saturn (7) in Libra, which is especially strong in Exalted position. Libra is also the eleventh (Luck) House from Lagna.

In relation to Tanu-kaset (Venus (6) in Libra), Capricorn is the fourth (Home) House that is related both to his mother and to his real estates. The Ruler of Capricorn is Saturn (7). Saturn (7) is in the eleventh (Luck) House from Lagna, the Special Position of Plenty and especially strong in Exalted position. This indicates a well to do and supportive family.

In relation to Tanu-kaset, the Sun (1) is the Ruler of the eleventh (Luck) House. It is in Libra, which is the eleventh (Luck) House from Lagna. This represents double luck, another indication of wealth. The Sun (1), the planet of honor, is in Fall position. This is perhaps the reason why he chose to build his business at the expense of his academic achievement. However, it is recovered by being with Tanu-kaset, giving him the ability to innovate.

Mercury (4) in Virgo is in both Ruler position and Exalted position, therefore especially strong, and gives him a good memory and intelligence. It is in conjunction with Mars (3), which is also in Perseverance position, making him hard working at finding new things, exploring new methods.

In relation to Tanu-kaset, Mars (3) is the Ruler of the second (Income) House. It is in Virgo, the tenth (Career) House from Lagna, in Perseverance position. It indicates work related to machinery and electronics, the nature of Mars (3).

In relation to Tanu-kaset, Rahu (8) is the Ruler of Aquarius, the fifth (Children) House that is related to speculation and financial luck. Rahu (8), the planet of gambling, is in the second (Income) House from Tanu-kaset, in Exalted position. This indicates money from speculation, financial investments in addition to his main line of business.

How long will his wealth continue?

Venus (6), Tanu-kaset, is surrounded by many strong and auspicious planets. In front there is Rahu (8) in Exalted position. In conjunction there is the recovered Sun (1) and Saturn (7) in

Exalted position. Behind there is Mars (3) in Perseverance position as well as Mercury (4) in both Ruler position and Exalted position. Wealth accumulation will just go on.

In relation to Tanu-kaset (Venus (6) in Libra), Jupiter (5) is the Ruler of the third (Friend) House. It is in Leo, the ninth (Exaltation) House from Lagna as well as the eleventh (Luck) House from Tanu-kaset. This indicates elder friends (the nature of Jupiter (5)), who give him advice and support.

Uranus (0) is in the tenth (Career) House from Tanu-kaset, indicating the ability to innovate, revolutionize and think out of the box, the nature of Uranus (0). This House is also related to his father, indicating that Uranus (0) may be affecting his father's health.

Mercury (4) is the Ruler of the ninth (Exaltation) House from Tanu-kaset. It is in the tenth (Career) House from Lagna, indicating important social work. Mercury (4) is also the Ruler of the twelfth (Loss) House from Tanu-kaset. It is in Virgo, the tenth (Career) House from Lagna. Its strong position intensifies the effect of loss. This indicates damage to certain parts of his work, some reduction to wealth and achievement short of his own targets. The twelfth House is also about secrecy. Perhaps this is why he went into retirement early; preferring to continue his work behind the scene.

His business launch of Windows
The birth chart of Bill Gates

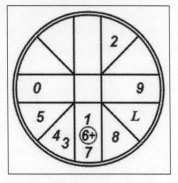

Thai astrology date: Saturday
Calendar Saturday 29 October 1955 at 11.57

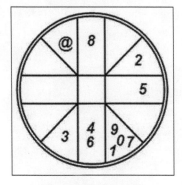

Planets in transit
on 20 November 1985

The big business breakthrough occurs at the age of 31. Between the ages of 29 and 32, the first (Self) House in transit, @, is in Taurus.

In the birth chart, in relation to @ in Taurus, Jupiter (5) is in the fourth House, the Special Position of Lotus, and indicating strong success. The Moon (2) in the birth chart is in the eleventh House from @, also the Special Position of Lotus. This double Special positions doubles the success while @ is in Taurus.

In the transit chart, Rahu (8) is opposite Saturn (7) in the birth chart, its Friendly Pair. Saturn (7) in transit is also in conjunction with Rahu (8) in the birth chart. This is important because they are the big planets, resulting in big luck.

In relation to @ in Taurus, Jupiter (5) is the Ruler of the eleventh (Luck) House. In the transit chart, Jupiter (5) is in the second (Income) House from Lagna, another indication of money success.

Among the indication by smaller planets, Mercury (4) is the Ruler of the second (income) House from @ in Taurus as well as the Ruler of the fifth (Children) House from @ in Taurus. In the transit chart, Mercury (4) is in the eleventh (Luck) House from Lagna, the Special Position. Venus (6), the Ruler of the first (Self) House from @, is also in the eleventh (Luck) House from Lagna.

His marriage
The birth chart of Bill Gates

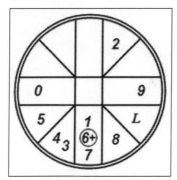

Thai astrology date: Saturday
Calendar Saturday 29 October 1955 at 11.57

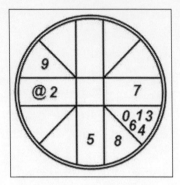

Planets in transit on 1 January 1994

His marriage occurs at age 39. Between the ages of 38 and 44, the first (Self) House is in Cancer.

In the birth chart, there is Venus (6) in the fourth House from @ in Cancer, the Special Position for Success, indicating success while @ is in Cancer. Saturn (7) is the Ruler of Capricorn, the seventh (Spouse) House from @. Saturn (7) is in conjunction with Venus (6). Spouse reaches success. In the birth chart, there is also Rahu (8) in the fifth House from @ in Cancer, also the Special Position of Plenty.

In the transit chart, Saturn (7) representing spouse and success is in the seventh (Spouse) House from @ in Cancer. It is strong in Ruler position. It can also reach Lagna, being in the Leading Engine position.

In relation to @ in Cancer, Jupiter (5) is the Ruler of the ninth (Exaltation) House. In the transit chart, Jupiter (5) is in the eleventh (Luck) House from Lagna. Honor is in the House of luck. This is also the Special Position of Plenty. Jupiter (5) is also in conjunction with the Sun (1) in the birth chart, its Friendly Pair.

In the birth chart, Venus (6) is in Libra, the fourth (Home) House in relation to @ in Cancer. It is also the Ruler of the eleventh (Luck) House from @ in Cancer. In the transit chart, Venus (6) is in conjunction with Lagna, and it is also in the Special Position of Plenty as well as in Perseverance position.

All the planets are auspicious for a happy and successful marriage.

Evita Peron

We believe this to be the birth chart of Evita Peron, wife of a President of Argentina, born on Wednesday 7 May 1919 at 05.00 near Buenos Aries, Argentina, GMT-03.00. She was married on 21 October 1945. Her husband was elected President in 1946 and 1951. She passed away on 26 July 1952.

We have not obtained official verification of the birth time, and therefore cannot claim without any doubt that this is her birth chart. We include her birth chart because it is a chart with birth location south of the equator.

The birth chart of Evita Peron

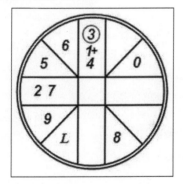

Thai astrology date: Wednesday
Calendar Wednesday 7 May 1919 at 15.00
Sunrise at 05.54

Lagna in Virgo indicates a gentle person, soft looking, easy to get along with all classes of people, intelligent, patient.

Mercury (4) is the Ruler of the first (Self) House. It is in the eighth (Death) House from Lagna. It indicates resettlement far away from the place of birth. But the planet representing self in the House of death also indicates serious illness or weak health.

The Sun (1) is Tanu-set. It shows a person with a good heart, pious, soft hearted, and eager to help others.

Mars (3) is Tanu-kaset. It is in Aries, the eighth (Death) House from Lagna. It reconfirms resettlement away from the birth place and weak health. Mars (3), Tanu-kaset, is in conjunction with the Sun (1), Tanu-set, and Mercury (4), the Ruler of the first (Self) House. This is the Result in High Position, indicating a leader, especially with the Sun (1) in Exalted position.

The Ruler of the fourth (Home) House from Tanu-kaset (Mars (3) in Aries), is the Moon (2). The fourth House represents father in a woman's birth chart. The Moon (2) is in the eleventh (Luck) House from Lagna, the Special Position of Lotus. It indicates a father that is well off and provides well for her childhood.

The Moon (2) in the Special Position also gives her high honor and position. However, there is Saturn (7) in Cancer in conjunction with the Moon (2) in the House of father. Saturn (7) is in Insecure position, indicating that her father's status is insecure. It affects his wealth and his health.

In relation to Tanu-kaset, Mars (3) in Aries, the tenth (Career) House is Capricorn, and the eleventh (Luck) House is Aquarius. Saturn (7) is the Ruler of both Houses. It is in Cancer, which is the eleventh (luck) House from Lagna. It indicates the ability for hard work, heavy responsibility, the character of Saturn (7). Saturn (7) also signifies support from the masses, the general public, and the grass roots people.

Mars (3) can reach the Moon (2), the troublesome pair of romance. Mars (3) as Tanu-kaset represents self. The Moon (2) is in sextile with Lagna, and therefore can reach self. This indicates the possibility of someone with more than one spouse, or someone willing to be the second spouse to another person.

In relation to Tanu-kaset (Mars (3) in Aries), the eighth (Death) House is Scorpio. Its Ruler is Mars (3), which is also Tanu-kaset. Its position in Aries is also the eighth (Death) House from Lagna. By Taksa, Mars (3) also represents Kali, and it is strong in Ruler position. This indicates a really big risk to her health. The risk is increased by Rahu (8), a Malificent planet, in Scorpio where Mars (3) is the Ruler. Rahu (8) in Scorpio can, therefore, influence Mars (3) regardless of the zodiac sign Mars (3) is in. The combination of Mars (3) and Rahu (8) indicates the risk related to cancer, or illness affecting the kidney or the liver or other internal organs.

In relation to Tanu-kaset, the seventh (Spouse) House is Libra. Its Ruler is Venus (6), the planet of beauty and romance, which is strong in Ruler position in Taurus. Taurus is also the ninth (Exaltation) House from Lagna. This indicates beauty and charm. The Moon (2), also signifying beauty, is in sextile with Venus (6), enhancing beauty.

Rahu (8), the planet of giant and power, is strong in Exalted position in Scorpio. It is opposite to Venus (6). It not only elevates the level of her beauty, but also indicates a person with more than one spouse (Venus (6) represents love). Each spouse is in high position, in authority.

In relation to Tanu-kaset (Mars (3) in Aries), the ninth (Exaltation) House is Sagittarius. Its Ruler is Jupiter (5), which is in Gemini. In relation to Lagna, Gemini is the tenth (Career) House. This indicates a career related to administration, politics or philanthropy. However, Jupiter (5) is in Insecure position. Her work does not reach the set goal.

By Taksa, Saturn (7) represents age; the indicator of longevity. It is in Insecure position, indicating the risk to health.

Her marriage to Juan Peron
The birth chart of Evita Peron

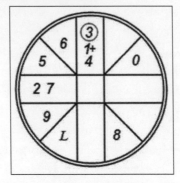

Thai astrology date: Wednesday
Calendar Wednesday 7 May 1919 at 15.00

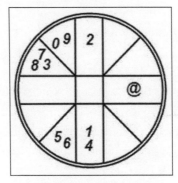

**Chart of planets in transit
on 21 October 1945**

The marriage to Juan Peron occurs at the age of 27. Between the ages of 26 and 32 years, the first (Self) House in transit, @, is in Capricorn.

While @ is in Capricorn, Saturn (7), the Ruler of Capricorn, represents self. In the birth chart, Saturn (7) is in Cancer, which is the seventh (Spouse) House from @ in Capricorn. The planet representing self is in the House of spouse.

While @ is in Capricorn, Cancer represents spouse. Because

the Moon (2) transits very quickly, for analysis of planet in transit, Saturn (7) is also used as the Ruler of Cancer in addition to the Moon (2). In the transit chart, Saturn (7) which represents spouse is in conjunction with Rahu (8), it's Friendly Pair, thus making Saturn (7) especially strong.

In the birth chart, Rahu (8) is in Scorpio. While @ is in Capricorn, Scorpio is the eleventh (Luck) House; therefore, Rahu (8) also represents luck. The two planets that represent luck and spouse are in conjunction with each other in the transit chart, indicating marriage to someone with power and influence, the nature of Rahu (8).

In the transit chart, there is also Jupiter (5) in Virgo in conjunction with Lagna. By Taksa in transit that year, Jupiter (5) represents Success. The planet in transit representing Success has reached self.

Her death
The birth chart of Evita Peron

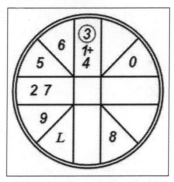

Thai astrology date: Wednesday
Calendar Wednesday 7 May 1919 at 15.00

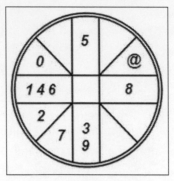

**Chart of planets in transit
on 26 July 1952**

Her death occurs at age 34. Between the ages of 33 and 37, the first (Self) House in transit, @, is in Aquarius. In the birth chart, @ is in conjunction with Uranus (0), the planet of sudden loss. Uranus (0) is strong because it is the Ruler in its own House. This shows the first risk.

While @ is in Aquarius, a Human sign, Saturn (7) in transit is the Special Omen planet. In the birth chart, Saturn (7) is in Cancer. In relation to @ in Aquarius, Cancer is now the sixth (Enemy) House. This shows the weakness in the birth chart. When @ transits into Aquarius, the position of Saturn (7) is especially adverse. By Taksa in transit, in that year Saturn (7) also represents Kali, making it especially dangerous.

While @ is in Aquarius, both Saturn (7) and Rahu (8) represent self in transit. In the transit chart, Saturn (7) is in the eighth (Death) House from @ in Aquarius. Rahu (8) is in the twelfth (Loss) House from @ in Aquarius.

In the transit chart, Saturn (7), representing enemy and Kali in transit and also the Special Omen planet, is in conjunction with Lagna.

Finally, in relation to @ in Aquarius, the eighth (Death) House is Virgo. The Ruler of Virgo is Mercury (4). In the transit chart, Mercury (4) is in Cancer in conjunction with Venus (6), the water

Element Pair. They are in the Cardinal sign of water element, hence making Mercury (4), representing death, especially strong. In the transit chart, Mercury (4) in Cancer can reach Lagna in sextile. The planet representing death reaches self.

John F Kennedy

We believe this to be the birth chart of John F Kennedy, born on Tuesday 29 May 1917 at 15.17 in Brookline, Massachusetts, USA, GMT-05.00. He was married on 12 September 1953 and had children in 1957 and 1960. He was elected President in 1960 and was assassinated on 22 November 1963.

We have not obtained official verification of the birth time, and therefore cannot claim without any doubt that this is his birth chart.

The birth chart of John F Kennedy

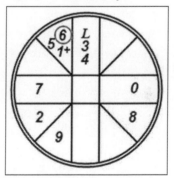

Thai astrology date: Tuesday
Calendar Wednesday 30 May 1917 at 03.17
Sunrise at 05.49

Lagna in Aries indicates a man of courage; he is strong built, sincere, dedicated, straight forward and prepared to make sacrifices.

Tanu-set is the Sun (1), which signifies a kind and pious man who likes to help others.

Tanu-kaset is Venus (6). It is in Ruler position in Taurus in conjunction with Tanu-set, the Sun (1), giving the Result in High Ability. It makes him daring, determined, purposeful.

In relation to Lagna, the ninth (Exaltation) House is Sagittarius. The Ruler of Sagittarius is Jupiter (5), which is in conjunction with Tanu-kaset in Taurus, the Result in High Exaltation. This indicates high political success. By Taksa, Jupiter (5) also represents Success.

In relation to Tanu-kaset (Venus (6) in Taurus), the fourth (Home) House of family is Leo. Its Ruler is the Sun (1), which is in conjunction with Tanu-kaset and is a Leading Engine of Lagna. This shows a good relationship with his family.

In relation to Tanu-kaset, the tenth (Career) House of father is Aquarius. Its Ruler is Rahu (8), which is in Sagittarius, the ninth (Exaltation) House from Lagna. This shows a supportive father of high society.

In relation to Tanu-kaset (Venus (6) in Taurus), Saturn (7) is the Ruler of both the ninth (Exaltation) House and the tenth (Career) House. Saturn (7) is in Cancer, the fourth (Home) House from Lagna. It indicates a career set by family. However, Saturn (7) in Insecure position makes it insecure.

What indicates the risk of assassination?

Examine all the three Malefic Houses from Tanu-kaset. In relation to Tanu-kaset (Venus (6) in Taurus), the eighth (Death) House is Sagittarius, whose Ruler is Jupiter (5). Jupiter (5) is both the Leading Engine of Lagna and the planet of Result in High Exaltation. The planet of death can reach self, and it is also the planet of honor. This explains why death occurs in a high career position.

In relation to Tanu-kaset, the sixth (Enemy) House is Libra, whose Ruler is Venus (6). Venus (6) is in Taurus as Tanu-kaset. The planet of enemy is the planet of self, another weakness. In relation to Tanu-kaset, the twelfth (Loss) House is Aries, whose Ruler is Mars (3). Therefore, Mars (3) represents loss and double cross. Mars (3) is strong in its Ruler position in Aries. Mars (3) is in conjunction with Lagna. The planet of loss reaches self.

Both Mars (3) and Rahu (8) are the planets that represent weapons. Rahu (8) is in Sagittarius, in trine with Lagna, adding to the risk of injury from weaponry.

His presidential election
The birth chart of John F Kennedy

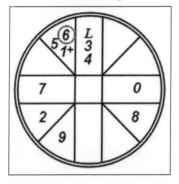

Thai astrology date: Tuesday
Calendar Wednesday 30 May 1917 at 03.17

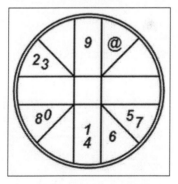

**Chart of planets in transit
on 8 November 1960**

His presidential election occurs at the age of 44. Between the ages of 40 and 44, the first (Self) House in transit, @, is in Pisces.

In the birth chart, in relation to @ in Pisces, the ninth (Exaltation) House is Scorpio. Its Ruler is Mars (3). In the birth chart, Mars (3) is in Aries, in Ruler position, and is the Leading Engine of @; therefore, auspicious for the person while @ is in Pisces.

In the birth chart, Venus (6) is in strong Ruler position in Taurus. In relation to @ in Pisces, Venus (3) is in the third House, the Special Position of Lotus, another indication of success.

In relation to @ in Pisces, the eleventh (Luck) House is Capricorn. Its Ruler is Saturn (7). In the birth chart, Saturn (7) is in Cancer, and Cancer is now the fifth House from @. This House represents sudden luck. Saturn (7) in the fifth House is also the Special Position of Plenty for @ in Pisces, an Aquatic sign.

In the transit chart, Jupiter (5), the Ruler of @ in Pisces and the Ruler of the tenth (Career) House from @ in Pisces is in Sagittarius, the ninth (Exaltation) House from Lagna. It is also strong in Ruler position.

In the transit chart, Saturn (7), the Ruler of the eleventh (Luck) House from @ in Pisces is also in Sagittarius, the ninth (Exaltation) House from Lagna, and another indication.

His assassination
The birth chart of John F Kennedy

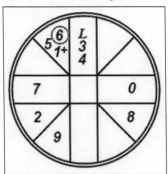

Thai astrology date: Tuesday
Calendar Wednesday 30 May 1917 at 03.17

254

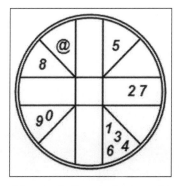

**Chart of planets in transit
on 22 November 1963**

His assassination occurs at the age of 47. Between the ages of 47
and 48, the first (Self) House in transit, @, is in Taurus.

In the birth chart, @ in Taurus is in conjunction with Jupiter
(5) and Venus (6). In relation to @ in Taurus, Jupiter (5) is the
Ruler of Sagittarius, the eighth (Death) House and Venus (6) is
the Ruler of Libra, the sixth (Enemy) House. Death and enemy
reach self.

In the birth chart, @ in Taurus is reached by two Maleficent
planets. It is in sextile with Saturn (7) and in trine with Uranus
(0), another weakness.

In the transit chart, @ in Taurus has Mars (3) in the opposite
sign. In relation to @ in Taurus, Mars (3) is the Ruler of the
twelfth (Loss) House. The planet representing loss can reach self.
Mars (3) is especially damaging because Taksa in transit that year
Mars (3) represents Kali.

In the transit chart, @ in Taurus also has Mercury (4) and
Venus (6) in the opposite sign. In the birth chart, Mercury (4) is
in Aries, the twelfth (Loss) House from @ in Taurus. Venus (6) is
the Ruler of Libra, the sixth (Enemy) House from @ in Taurus.
The planets that represent loss and enemy reach self.

Finally, in the transit chart, there is Rahu (8) in Gemini. It is
now the Leading Engine of @ in Taurus. In the birth chart, Rahu

(8) is in Sagittarius, the eighth (Death) House from @ in Taurus. The planet representing death reaches self.

Osama Bin Laden

We believe this to be the birth chart of Osama Bin Laden, the biggest name terrorist in recent years. He was born on Sunday 10 March 1957 at 10.28 in Jeddah, Saudi Arabia, GMT+03.00. He was married in 1974. He organized one of the biggest terrorist attacks in the USA on 11 September 2001.

We have no official information of the birth time, and therefore cannot claim without any doubt that this is his birth chart.

The birth chart of Osama Bin Laden

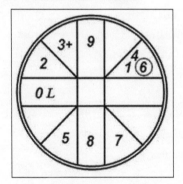

Thai astrology date: Sunday
Calendar Sunday 10 March 1957 at 14.28
Sunrise at 06.00

Lagna in Cancer normally indicates a gentle, peace loving person who likes looking after other people. However, the Moon (2), the Ruler of the first (Self) House is in Gemini, the twelfth (Loss) House. This causes him to have strange, unconventional thoughts, and unusual convictions. Uranus (0), the planet of rebellion and sudden calamity, is in conjunction with Lagna, adding to the antisocial nature.

Mars (3) is Tanu-set, indicating a non compromising person who wants to win always, a hard headed person. Mars (3) is in both Insecure position and Assistance position, giving occasional wins.

Venus (6) is Tanu-kaset. It is in Aquarius, the eighth (Death) House from Lagna, indicating resettlement far away from his birth place, or someone who lives out of sight.

The Sun (1) and Mercury (4) are in conjunction with Tanu-kaset, giving the Result in High Leadership. This enables him to be a strong leader of his group.

In Libra, the fourth (Home) House from Lagna, there is Rahu (8) in Assistance position. It indicates a well to do family that gives him support during his youth. Rahu (8) is in the ninth (Exaltation) House from Tanu-kaset, Venus (6) in Aquarius. This indicates good education abroad.

In relation to Tanu-kaset (Venus (6) in Aquarius), the tenth (Career) House is Scorpio whose Ruler is Mars (3). Mars (3) is in Taurus, the eleventh (Luck) House from Lagna, in Assistance position. It indicates good family support at the beginning. But Mars (3) in Insecure position says that the support is not permanent.

In relation to Tanu-kaset, the twelfth (Loss) House is Capricorn whose Ruler is Saturn (7). Saturn (7) representing loss and secrecy is in the fifth (Children) House from Lagna. Saturn (7) is in Assistance position, and also the Special Position of Plenty. This indicates a life full of secret activities, loss of lives and the ability to recruit followers. There are several successes too. However, it also means that his followers fall away one by one.

Jupiter (5), the planet of morality and justice, is in Insecure position, thus has its good quality reduced. It leads to unconventional reasoning and unusual priorities.

In relation to Tanu-kaset, Jupiter (5) is the Ruler of the second (Income) House and the eleventh (Luck) House. Jupiter (5) in

Virgo is the third (Friend) House from Lagna, indicating that he relies on financial support from his relatives and close friends. However, Jupiter (5) in Insecure position means that the support can die away.

Saturn (7) in the fifth (Children) House from Lagna is the Special Position of Hardship, indicating a separation or disagreement with his children.

In relation to Tanu-kaset, the sixth (Enemy) House is Cancer. Its Ruler is the Moon (2). The Moon (2) is in the twelfth (Loss) House from Lagna, making him safe from his enemy.

In relation to Tanu-kaset, the eighth (Death) House is Virgo. Its Ruler is Mercury (4). Mercury (4) is in the eighth (Death) House from Lagna. It indicates a man that cannot be easily put down. Mercury (4) is together with its water Element Pair, Venus (6). They are especially strong because they are in a water element sign. Furthermore, Venus (6) is the Ruler of Libra, the ninth (Exaltation) House from Tanu-kaset. These factors point to the ability to keep on hiding, surviving and continuing to lead.

Although you may not hear from this man, you cannot readily write him off.

The 911 event
The birth chart of Osama Bin Laden

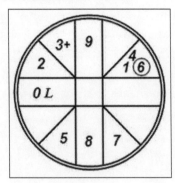

Thai astrology date: Sunday
Calendar Sunday 10 March 1957 at 14.28

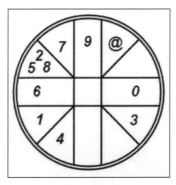

**Chart of Planets in transit
on 9 September 2001**

The tragic event occurs at age 45. Between the ages of 41 and 46, the first (Self) House in transit, @, is in Pisces.

In relation to @ in Pisces, the Ruler of the first (Self) House is Jupiter (5). Therefore, while @ is in Pisces, Jupiter (5) represents self. In the birth chart, Jupiter (5) is in Virgo in Insecure position. Self in Insecure position indicates unusual or improper thoughts while @ is in Pisces.

In relation to @ in Pisces, the twelfth (Loss) House is Aquarius. Its Co-Ruler is Saturn (7). Therefore, while @ is in Pisces, Saturn (7) represents loss. In the birth chart, Saturn (7) is in Scorpio, which is the ninth (Exaltation) House from @. The planet of loss and secret plots interferes with the House of morality.

In relation to @ in Pisces, the sixth (Enemy) House is Leo. Its Ruler is the Sun (1). Therefore, while @ is in Pisces, the Sun (1) represents enemy. In the birth chart, the Sun (1) is in Aquarius, which is the twelfth (Loss) House from @. The planet of enemy is trapped in the House of loss. The three indications in the birth chart show a strong chance of his plot succeeding while @ is in Pisces.

In the transit chart, Jupiter (5) is in Gemini, the fourth House from @, and in the Special Position of Success for people with

Lagna in Pisces, an Aquatic sign. It indicates success. Jupiter (5) is also with Rahu (8), the Ruler of Aquarius, the twelfth (Loss) House of secret plots.

In relation to @ in Pisces, the twelfth (Loss) House is Aquarius. Its Co-Ruler is Saturn (7) which transits into Taurus, the eleventh (Luck) House from Lagna. The planet representing loss and secret plot is in the House of luck.

In relation to @ in Pisces, the ninth (Exaltation) House is Scorpio. Its Ruler is Mars (3) which transits into Sagittarius, the sixth (Enemy) House from Lagna. The planet representing morality and goodness is captured in the House of enemy.

Further risk?
The birth chart of Osama Bin Laden

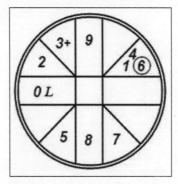

Thai astrology date: Sunday
Calendar Sunday 10 March 1957 at 14.28

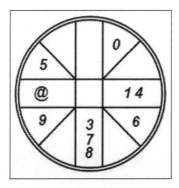

Chart of Planets in transit
between 1-13 February 2014

We sincerely hope that there is nothing like 911 ever again. However, we think it is best to be on guard and beware of any possible risk. The person with Mars (3) as Tanu-set does not give up easily.

We see a planet pattern that can be considered as a risk in 2014. In that year his age is 57. Between the ages of 57 and 62, the first (Self) House in transit, @, is in Cancer.

In the birth chart, Jupiter (5) is in Insecure position. While @ is in Cancer, the sixth (Enemy) House is Sagittarius whose Ruler is Jupiter (5). Therefore, Jupiter (5) represents enemy. Having his enemy weak in Insecure position is the first indication.

In the transit chart, Jupiter (5), the planet of enemy, is in Gemini, the twelfth (Loss) House from Lagna. The enemy is further weakened in the House of loss.

Finally, in the transit chart, there are Mars (3), Saturn (7) and Rahu (8) in Libra. All three planets are in the Special Position of Plenty for Lagna in Cancer, indicating exceptional chances of success. In relation to @ in Cancer, Mars (3) is also the Ruler of Aries, the tenth (Career) House. The planet representing work is especially strong between the 1st and 13th February 2014.

This is the one event that we hope will not happen, but it is better to be forewarned.

Epilogue

Be sure to keep a note of the main events happening to you from now on in order to compare them to the movement of the planets. The more observations, the more you learn.

Finally, we wish to repeat that the best way to use this book is to discover your strengths and weaknesses to improve yourself. Remember that the an astrological prediction only shows an inclination. The positive prediction will come true only with effort, and the negative prediction can still be modified. A weakness in character can, with patience, be changed. For example, the person who has the Moon (2) in the third House from Rahu (8) has the risk of being too soft hearted and gullible to call for help from friends and acquaintances. He/she can try to overcome this habit by starting a collection of something, stamps, coins or dolls. By building attachment to the collection over time, he will gradually lessen the risk of the Moon (2) in the third House from Rahu (8).

May the planets enlighten your way forever!

Appendix - Summary of the main charts

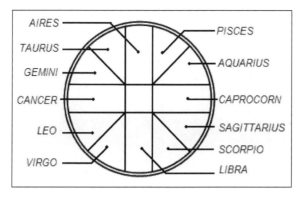

Name of the signs

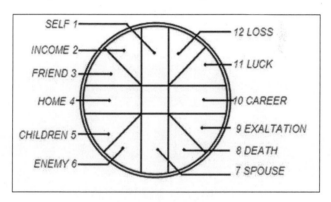

Numbering of the Houses

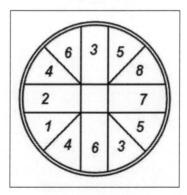

Ruler of each sign

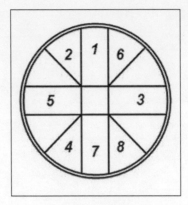

Exalted positions

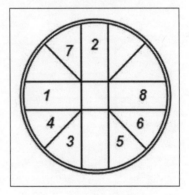

Perseverance positions

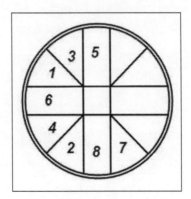

Assistance positions

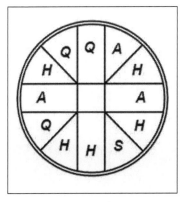

Grouping of signs

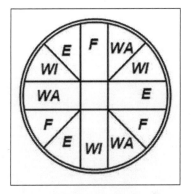

Element of signs

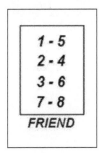

Friendly Pairs

Enemy Pairs

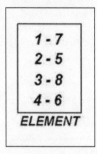

Element Pairs

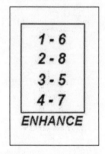

Enhancement Pairs

About the Authors

Mr. Thirachai Phuvanatnaranubala

(born 1951) studied economics at the London School of Economics and qualified as a Chartered Accountant in England. He was Deputy Governor of the central bank in Thailand before becoming the Secretary General and Chairman of the Capital Market Supervisory Board of the Thai Securities and Exchange Commission. He took up Thai astrology as a side interest, became totally immersed in the subject and came up with the idea of spreading this useful knowledge to the world.

Mr. Kornaek Khongpurttiroj

(born 1972) studied Business management in Thailand for his first degree. His interest in Thai astrology began during his undergraduate years. Through his study and practice of over 15 years, he explored many approaches to Thai astrology, and narrowed down to the method used in this book. It is simple to follow and can be readily applied by most readers.

BOOKS

O is a symbol of the world, of oneness and unity. In different cultures it also means the "eye," symbolizing knowledge and insight. We aim to publish books that are accessible, constructive and that challenge accepted opinion, both that of academia and the "moral majority."

Our books are available in all good English language bookstores worldwide. If you don't see the book on the shelves ask the bookstore to order it for you, quoting the ISBN number and title. Alternatively you can order online (all major online retail sites carry our titles) or contact the distributor in the relevant country, listed on the copyright page.

See our website www.o-books.net for a full list of over 500 titles, growing by 100 a year.

And tune in to myspiritradio.com for our book review radio show, hosted by June-Elleni Laine, where you can listen to the authors discussing their books.

MySpiritRadio